LIVING WITH YOUR LAND

LIVING

Bulletin 53
Cranbrook Institute of Science, 1968

WITH YOUR LAND

*A Guide to Conservation for
the City's Fringe*

by John Vosburgh

CREDITS

Grateful acknowledgment is made to Harper & Bros., New York, for the following excerpts from *Living Ideas in America,* edited by Henry Steele Commager, 1951:

From *The Significance of the Frontier,* by Frederick Jackson Turner (page 1).

From *The Land,* by Henry Steele Commager (page 7).

From *From Plymouth Rock to Ducktown,* by Stuart Chase (page 10).

And to Holt, Rinehart and Winston, New York, for the quotation (page 7).

from *The Quiet Crisis,* by Stewart L. Udall, 1965.

And to McGraw-Hill Book Co., New York, for the quotation (page 16) from *Conserving Natural Resources,* by Shirley W. Allen, 1955.

And to Columbia University Press, New York, for the quotation (page 11) from *Man and Nature in America,* by Arthur A. Ekirch, Jr., 1963.

And to Verne E. Davison, Regional Biologist, Soil Conservation Service, U.S. Department of Agriculture, Portland, Oregon; and Thomas Y. Crowell Co., New York, for the bird feeding and nesting material, page 70. This material appeared in *Audubon Magazine,* September-October 1964, July–August 1965, and November–December 1966, and in book form in *Attracting Birds: from the Prairies to the Atlantic,* 1966.

Drawings

The illustrations are from drawings by Mr. Matthew Kalmenoff, with the exception of the following: page 48, Ruth Powell Brede; page 96, Vera K. Boardman; pages 86 and 94, Dudley M. Blakely; page 111, David T. Crothers.

Photographs

No. 1, R.G. Askew; 2–5, 13, Soil Conservation Service; 6–10, U.S. Department of Agriculture; 11, Eastern Michigan Tourist Association; 12, 14–18, 20, 21, R.B. Fisher; 19, 22, Robert T. Hatt.

Publisher's Foreword

The members of the Garden Club of Michigan, in response to our suggestion, provided funds for the preparation of a small book to serve as a guide for persons freshly exposed to life at the city's fringe; and others perhaps longer there, newly awakened to man's responsibility to his environment, who seek advice on the physical and biological problems encountered next door to nature.

This book is the product of that sponsorship. It is a book for people who live beyond sidewalks, but who are neither farmers nor lumbermen. It will have little to offer the person who lives in a subdivision in which there are six houses per acre.

It cannot answer all questions, for circumstances differ and circumstances change. The tremendous complexity of the biological network through which one form of life is dependent on the existence of another makes no answer simple. And the great diversity of conditions found in the northeastern quarter of our country makes full coverage impractical in a book of this size. Often there is no completely satisfactory answer to conservation problems; at any rate none practical for the individual land holder or the community of neighbors to apply. The problem may be regional in dimension and require a regional attack.

Yet for those who would derive enjoyment from the natural values of their land, and who would want to preserve these values for future generations, this book should prove a helpful guide.

The author, John Vosburgh, is a writer with the National Park Service, Department of the Interior, where he is chief of the Branch of Features and General Inquiries, Office of Information. He was editor of *Audubon Magazine,* 1961–1966.

Matthew Kalmenoff, who furnished most of the drawings for this book, is a staff artist of The American Museum of Natural History. The other artists were at one time or another on the staff of the Institute.

Cranbrook Institute of Science

Acknowledgments

Deserving of much gratitude are the many scientists, historians, planners, conservationists, and other authors whose writings were consulted. Especially helpful were publications of the Soil Conservation Service, United States Department of Agriculture; the USDA Yearbooks of 1963, 1958 and 1957, and other USDA publications.

Thanks are due also to Dr. William T. Gillis, Michigan State University, for data on poison ivy; Dr. Findlay E. Russell, Director of the Laboratory of Neurological Research, Los Angeles General Hospital, for his counsel on venomous snake bites; to Robert Froman of Garnersville, New York, for calling attention to important new material on spiders; to Dr. Monroe Coleman, 1965 Chairman, and to Dr. Eloise W. Kailin, 1964 Chairman, Committee on Insects, the American Academy of Allergy, for their data on insect stings.

Also to Dr. Joseph J. Shomon, Director, Nature Centers Division, and to Roland C. Clement, staff biologist, National Audubon Society, for their help on nature centers and hawks respectively; and to Les D. Line, of *Audubon Magazine,* for reading the manuscript in one of the early stages and making several helpful suggestions. A word of thanks is also fitting for Mrs. John Vosburgh, Mrs. Reuben Rabinovitch and Mrs. Emlyn Blue for their typing, and for Mrs. James V. Fletcher of Cranbrook Institute of Science for making necessary changes in the author's manuscript to keep the book updated and in accord with the ever-shifting environmental scene.

John Vosburgh
Bethesda, Maryland

Table of Contents

Introduction

The dominant fact of American life is movement, historian Frederick Jackson Turner observed. When he published this statement in 1893, the gasoline automobile was a novelty similar to a self-propelled flying suit of today. But the automobile soon verified Turner's judgment—probably beyond his wildest expectations.

Today the movement is from the country to the city and, on a greater scale, from the city to the suburbs. Even the continuing Westward Movement, of which Turner was the chief interpreter, lacks the scope and social implications of the current rush to the suburban countryside.

1

Every year a million acres of the American landscape near our urban centers give way to housing projects, shopping plazas, industry, and often to less useful man-made excrescences.

"The American energy will continually demand a wider field for its exercise," Turner said in marking the disappearance of the frontier. Our sprawling suburbs scribble their endorsement of this statement across the countryside, usually with unimaginative lines and haphazard growth.

The suburban movement may be somewhat prosaic compared with the settling of a continent and the winning of the West, but the number of its participants ranges in the tens of millions instead of in the thousands. Is it any wonder that many people find themselves strangers in the suburbs? The transition from an apartment in Detroit, Manhattan, Chicago, or Philadelphia to a suburban community may enrich the spirit of the new suburbanite but it does not automatically qualify him as an expert in his new environment. There is no training course for life in the urban fringe. You receive no diploma or instruction upon graduating from an urban apartment with janitor service and a doorman, to a suburban home with elm disease, crabgrass, and mosquitoes. Years of feeding pigeons on the city window ledge do not qualify a family and its descendants as experts on swifts in the suburban chimney, flying squirrels in the attic, or a mole in the lawn. Experience with city-reared parakeets doesn't help the fledgling suburbanite cope with a skunk in the garbage can.

All this is not to say that persons newly emerged from the city may not be wide-eyed at the new worlds around them, even enriched by them. They will learn quickly, but questions pile up quickly too. There's a wasp nest by the door. Is the snake in the woodpile dangerous? Songbirds are flying into the picture window. Green "worms" are dropping off the shade trees. The septic tank is overflowing. What do we do?

This book attempts to serve as a guide to appropriate action. Its objective is to furnish some light where nature meets the suburbs—and even a lantern is handy to have around.

There is enjoyment in the suburbs, in being close to wild animals, plants, and scenic beauty, but there are also responsibilities. Beyond the boundary fence are community problems, and of these I write. Americans are at the crossroads today—and not just at the shopping center crossroads.

Our suburban countryside will be what we make it. It can be a monotonous checkerboard of look-alike houses or a planned community of diversified homes. We can have scarred fields and hillsides or green landscapes and rolling woodlands. We can reach our suburban homes by way of billboard-lined, four-lane alleys featuring hot dog stands, neon signs, and honkytonks; or along winding parkways verdant in spring and summer, colorful in fall and winter, and rich in trees, grass, and shrubbery.

A fortunate few can still have acreage and elbow room. Astute minds are at work trying to assure us a higher quality environment. A significant effort was President Johnson's history-making bipartisan White House Conference on Natural Beauty, May 24, 1965.

"The technology which has given us everything from the computer to the teleprompter has created a hundred sources of blight," the President said. He cited "the uncontrolled growth in building, uninformed by the need to protect nature, unchecked by the citizens whose world is being blighted."

One Conference report said "urban sprawl creates a disorderly, impractical and unattractive mess," and blamed "the general failure to acquire open spaces ahead of metropolitan expansion. These spaces which would give the metropolitan area a unity, a dignity and a habitability, are chopped up and destroyed."

The report urged strengthened federal aid for open space acquisition, local planning and development. Another report suggested that states furnish nursery stock to landowners for an endless tree planting drive. Federal landscape grants to communities were advocated, to stimulate beautifying programs. An all-out attack on auto junkyards by federal, state, local government, and private sources was urged.

In 1965 President Johnson sent four Highway Beautification bills to Congress and accompanied them with a special message. Two bills sought to spur highway beautification by the states, one dealt with auto junkyards, and the other with billboards. This fourth bill called for restrictions on billboards within 1,000 feet of the highway right-of-way. The outdoor advertising cabal was ready. With roadside landowners, state and local highway authorities (more amenable to local pressures), and others who think more of the dollar than decency in roadside appearance, they rushed to the billboard barricades.

By the time the bill came up for vote, the 1,000-foot restriction had been reduced to 660 feet. The President's recommendation that a state be deprived of 100 percent of its federal highway aid if it didn't pass satisfactory billboard and junkyard legislation was changed beyond recognition. The act would penalize a state only 10 percent of its federal highway aid. Another new provision required the federal government (Mr. and Mrs. Taxpayer) to pay 75 percent of the "just compensation" for billboards and junkyards screened or removed. Just why the despoiler should be paid for removing the eyesore with which he violated the motorist's line of vision is not clear. Under the most generous reasoning, it would seem that anyone investing in a billboard or junkyard does so at his own risk. He, not the taxpayer, should bear the cost of removal.

In view of the powerful opposition to the bill, however, enactment of the Highway Beautification Act was a major achievement, even with its weakened provisions. It will make many suburban areas more attractive and livable. The story of this act is a good example of how democracy *can* improve the environment of its people—one milestone in man's endless quest for betterment.

So dubious are some planners of responsible leadership on the part of developers that they advocate the purchase of vacant fields by local government for speculative gain. Local government control of the purse strings for road, water, sewer, gas, and power facilities could assure the outcome of the speculation. The advantages are at least two-fold: (1) The success of the investment is likely to lower the taxpayer's burden. (2) The community thus can control the manner in which the land is developed. An attractive suburban area can be assured before the final bonanza sale to private developers.

A similar technique, also aimed at assuring a well-planned community, would allow city governments to create suburban development districts. Before the district could sell its raw land to developers it would insist on a far-sighted land use plan guaranteeing perpetuation of true natural charm. A variation of this idea would create a complete "new town," balancing commercial and industrial factors with residential needs and esthetic considerations before deeding it over to developers.

The Open Space Action Committee of New York began translating theory into action in 1965. This group attacked suburban problems, especially the need for open spaces, head-on. The well funded Committee mobilized its experts for action in 16 suburban counties of Metropolitan New York. This is one of the most significant non-governmental, non-commercial efforts to do something about the haphazard growth of our urban fringes where neatness of design and a concern for open space are rare commodities.

From 1950 to 1960 more than 1.5 million people moved to the suburbs of New York City. Some 6.5 million more are expected to join them by 1985. The country's other cities face similar outlying growth. Several million Americans thus will be enjoying the pleasures of suburbia for the first time in the Northeast, Middle Atlantic, and Midwest states. For both new and older suburbanites, this book is designed. May it prove a friendly introduction to the many faces of nature at the suburban doorstep.

Passenger pigeon

1. From Wilderness to Subdivision

Our jetliner was making its descent at John F. Kennedy International Airport. A passenger in an adjacent chair watched the passing sea and countryside. "Seems every time we come in over Long Island or Jersey, the suburbs extend farther out," he said, pointing through the window. "I can remember only a few years ago when that 20-mile built-up area on Long Island was all farmland."

With slight adjustment, his observations would hold true for the fringes of most of the country's booming cities. Urbanization of the countryside is not a new development but its dynamic tides are continually bringing new problems as well as happiness to both the individual and the community.

The trend to the suburbs was probably pre-ordained from the moment the first automobile took the road and provided a quick link between city and country. Now the spread of suburbia has become one of the great cultural, sociological, and economic developments of the 20th century. In their flight to the suburbs urban Americans hope to merge the conveniences of city life with the advantages of country life. Rural Americans, forced to the city for a livelihood, seek in the suburbs their lost values of the countryside coupled with the pay checks of the city.

New communities are born; villages that hadn't increased their populations by a single soul in 100 years are bulging with new neighborhoods —Woodland Estates, Forest Lawns, Town and Country's, and similar utopian manors.

In one sense, the expansion of suburbia with its waves of new communities and shopping centers is relatively new. In another sense, urbanization of the countryside is merely a new chapter in the old story of changing land use in progress ever since the first settlers began clearing the primeval forest.

Today's suburban home site was yesterday's cornfield. Yesterday's cornfield was a cow pasture until the farmer had to give up dairying for lack of farm hands. Before that the land was a cutover woodlot, and before that a subsistence homestead. Prior to the homestead it was possibly second growth forest that had sprung up after the original stand had been cut for timber, sailing ship masts, or fuel for colonial iron furnaces and for wood-burning locomotives.

The original forest often stretched to the ocean's edge—in places a dark, towering cover of green over hill and dale, interrupted only by the open oaklands, lakes, quiet rivers, Indian settlements, and burns. Most of the East was blanketed by one gigantic forest—virgin stands of oak, maple, ash, hickory, chestnut, tulip, pine, and other trees. Their massive girths reflected robust ages of as much as 400 to 500 years. The more whimsical settlers said a squirrel could travel from the East Coast to the Mississippi without touching ground. Today we would say that America then had wall-to-wall forests from the Atlantic to the prairies.

Colonial Americans viewed the forest lands much as a desert tribesman views the desert sands—limitless and beyond count. If some settlers were inspired by the solitude and immensity of the forest, others viewed the everlasting woods as a nuisance and a headache. The trees stood where crops should be growing and livestock grazing. Thus the forests had to go.

By axe, saw, fire, oxen, shoulder power, and horsepower, the land was cleared. The settlers often found they had more trees on their hands than they could dispose of. Then they held a log-burning, piling up the newly cut trees like stove wood and setting them ablaze.

"The virgin forests of North America were among the masterpieces of the natural world," Stewart L. Udall has said in *The Quiet Crisis.* "Europe had hardly a dozen tree types. The American expanse had more than a hundred, and our many soils and climate zones produced the largest and oldest trees on any continent."

The destruction of most of this forest wonderland within a few generations after introduction of the circular saw early in the 19th century has awed and fascinated historians, economists, and sociologists.

"Never before in recorded history," said historian Henry Steele Commager, "had so spacious and rich an area been thrown open to man. . . In a sense, the incomparable richness of the continent, the variety and the accessibility of its resources went to the collective head of the American people. There was land enough, said Thomas Jefferson in 1801, for our descendants 'to the thousandth and thousandth generation' . . . Yet within only three generations the Census Bureau could announce the disappearance of the frontier line, and within another generation the problem of conservation of land itself became acute."

In less than 350 years the young nation cut 198 million acres of its primeval forest—an area as large as the total land and water surface of New England, New York, Pennsylvania, Ohio, Maryland, Virginia, and North Carolina. Often wastefully and often unwisely, to nurture a new and demanding civilization, the settlers and timber men reduced the 822 million acres of dense forest in the 48 coterminous states to 623,828,000 by 1946. Wooded acreage had increased to 636.3 million by January 1, 1965, thanks to reforestation and rural population movement to the cities.

Precious little of our forest acreage has never been touched by axe or saw. The U.S. Forest Service has no "virgin timber" category but classifies 8 percent of our 508,845,000 acres of commercial forest land (including Alaska's and Hawaii's) as "old-growth." Some of the old-growth stands, all in the West, are entirely virgin timber, as is most of Alaska's 119 million forest acres.

In the tranquil, sylvan world of colonial America, fire, storm, and insects struck the forests even as they did after the advent of the white man; but nature could absorb the impact. If fire occurred from lightning or other natural causes, nature produced another forest. The trees protected the soil from wind and rain erosion. Countless forms of wild-life, microscopic animal life, and plant life, acting as part of nature's self-sustaining cycle, kept the forest floor matted with layers of humus which retained and regulated water levels. From the grubs in the decaying plant and animal matter, and the one-celled plant life around them, to the American Indian himself, an ecological network of interdependent organisms held nature in balance.

The forests also provided a haven for bird life, beneficial insects, and other animals active in controlling infestations of pest insects. The gypsy moth, an imported pest, had not yet made its entry on the scene, and chemical pesticides capable of destroying nature's balance were still 300 years away. If an occasional insect devastation occurred, nature in time produced its own remedy or complete atonement.

The westward waves of settlers found a wilderness not only unexploited but unpolluted as well. To drink from the lakes and streams was as natural as breathing. It seemed impossible, even in the early 20th century, that man could ever taint or exhaust the boundless supply of fresh water. The country seemed blessed with springs that never ran dry. Unslashed by man, the forests provided a canopy of leaves and branches that kept out the sunshine, preventing the evaporation of moisture and retaining the water level. Just one river, the Niagara, poured 500,000 tons of crystal pure water over its falls every minute.

These were not muddy flood waters—our rivers had not yet become muddy channels of silt—but the nature-regulated runoff of the land. The forests held the hillside soils in their grip, allowing runoff with little soil loss. Man had not yet so altered the balance of nature that the country would lose three billion tons of soil a year to wind and water erosion—as it was later to do. He had not yet denuded the hillsides and poured the filth of his sewers and factories into the breeding streams of the trout, salmon, and shad.

The Hudson, the Connecticut, the Potomac, the Ohio, Mississippi, Wisconsin, Au Sable, and Manistee rivers were clear and stenchless. Some prairie rivers carried large quantities of silt during floods, but the mud-carrying days of the Mississippi that lay ahead probably have never been matched. Man had not yet mutilated the grasslands of the Great Plains and the prairies and the watersheds of the Ohio, the Missouri, and the Mississippi. By the 1930s, however, the Father of Waters would be dumping 400 million tons of soil per year into the Gulf of Mexico. To transport such a load by freight car would require a train 63,300 miles long—or sufficient to stretch around the earth more than two and a half times at the equator.

The early settlers found a variety and abundance of wildlife. Some animals were essential to many colonists' survival, providing food, clothing, and trading materials. But others were a possible threat to livestock. To safeguard their herds and flocks, colonists were known to trap timber wolves in pits, then jump in and club the animals to death.

By 1856, forms of wildlife which Henry Thoreau called "the nobler animals"— the wolf, mountain lion, bear, moose, deer, wolverine, wild turkey, and beaver—had been exterminated from his home area around Concord. In the West, one of the most wanton hunting campaigns in history wiped out more than 99.99 percent of the 15 million bison (commonly called buffalo) that once roamed the Great Plains. Late in the 19th century only 550 survived.

The plentiful and colorful Carolina parakeet, the United States' only parrot, was virtually wiped out by the early 20th century, although one flock was reported in 1920 and another as late as the 1930s. The passenger pigeon, which once blotted out the sun with its massive flights, was extinct by 1914. Only a century earlier Alexander Wilson, the frontier ornithologist, had reported a single flight of passenger pigeons a mile wide and 240 miles long, containing an estimated two billion birds. And the bald eagle population has fallen sharply in recent years. The National Audubon Society reports not more than 5,000 in the 48 coterminous states, although Alaska still has eagles in abundance.

Beaver were trapped and hunted in such numbers that their skins were used for currency. Companies were founded and fortunes established merely in marketing beaver skins and shipping hundreds of thousands of pelts to Europe. Even our fish resources declined. The Atlantic salmon disappeared as a commercial item, and commercial catches of haddock and lobsters have fallen sharply. The sea lampreys, entering the Great Lakes through more recently man-made channels, have all but wiped out the lake trout as a food item.

In recent years thoughtful men have been taking a second look at campaigns to eliminate predatory animals such as coyotes, mountain lions, timber wolves, foxes, owls, and hawks. Farmers have learned that owls and hawks are their best rat traps and that 75 percent of some owls' food consists of rodents. The much-maligned fox consumes so many insects and rodents that its occasional seizure of a chicken is a small price to pay for the service. It has been found that a prevalence of rodents often results if coyotes and foxes are killed off.

Such an understanding attitude, however, was unknown in colonial times. The early Americans were overwhelmed by the wealth of resources before them. If nature stood in the way of enjoyment of these riches, man would have to conquer nature, and he set out to do so.

There were exceptions. The Quakers and Mormons, for example, felt they had a God-given responsibility to save the natural resources as well as to exploit them. William Penn was probably the only man of influence in colonial times who understood the danger of misusing nature. In building Philadelphia, Penn not only sought to avoid the congestion that plagued New York and Boston but planned to do something about protecting the countryside also. He insisted that Philadelphia be laid out with large, open squares so as to keep the city "a greene country towne." Of even more importance, Penn required that one of every six acres be left uncut.

Perceptive men such as William Penn and Henry Thoreau were far outnumbered and outshouted by the so-called empire builders, however. The "manifest destiny" of the empire builders was not to be stifled by philosophic tracts or farming principles—not for a while at least. Not until men of courage and action—Carl Schurz, Gifford Pinchot, and Theodore Roosevelt—began swinging their nightsticks from Washington.

Carl Schurz, a German-born conservationist and a senator from Wisconsin, became Secretary of the Interior under President Rutherford B. Hayes in 1877. Alarmed at the rapacity with which the public domain was being seized by mineral, railroad, cattle, and lumber interests, Schurz moved to halt the onrush. Immediately he was maligned. Schurz's ideas, cried his foes, were clearly "foreign" and "un-American." The Secretary was not easily deterred, however, and exposed some of the timber barons and what they were doing to the public lands. Though the tremendous economic power of the opposition slowed up his crusade, Schurz had sounded the alarm. Twelve years later he was still sounding it, and men like Gifford Pinchot and Roosevelt were listening.

By 1936 Stuart Chase could draw up a shocking balance sheet of our plundered resources, adding a forest category of his own: "Cut-over, burned-over lands are still called 'forest' on the maps," he said, "but we see that almost 100 million acres are really dead land—totally unknown in the old America." Much of the cutover land has been put to use since Chase wrote this, of course. Hunting, fishing, camping, and skiing have proved appropriate for such areas in Michigan, Wisconsin, and other cutover states.

Perhaps the most encouraging sign on the conservation horizon today is the growing realization that some unscrupulous characters stole many of Uncle Sam's prize resource horses before the barn door was locked, but that it must not happen again.

"No other nation," says Arthur A. Ekirch, Jr. "has equaled the American people in their paradoxical ability to devastate the natural world and at the same time mourn its passing."

The time for mourning, however, can also be a time for mobilizing. We know the follies of the past, and can plan more intelligently for the future. Each of us in the suburbs has a personal stake in a healthy, pleasant, constructive community. We can help to safeguard that stake by learning to understand nature at our doorsteps and to come to friendly terms with it.

In the group above are shown (1) ant, (2) harvestman (or daddy longlegs), (3) millipede (or thousand legs), (4) springtail, (5) sowbug, (6) rove beetle, (7) earthworm, (8) slug, (9) acorn weevil. No. (10) slime mold (a plant).

2. *The Site and the Soil*

If you move to the suburbs, you'll probably take great care to select the type of house and neighborhood you prefer. You'll check the mortgage payments, the taxes, insurance, schools, fire and police protection. But will you be equally dutiful in checking the quality of the soil, the drainage, erosion tendencies, and vegetation? You may get the colonial design or split-level home you want at the right price, but a poorly chosen site can prove costly. Your hillside may afford a fine view and appear as solid as Gibralter while the real estate agent is showing the property. Yet the very soil under his feet may be so porous and weak that house and driveway will settle into it. And what assurance do you have that your steeply terraced, freshly planted lawn won't wash away in a few heavy rains? Despite newly planted shrubs and saplings, will your lot, robbed of natural vegetation by the bulldozer, give you the summer shade, winter windbreak, atmosphere, and bird life you have a right to expect in country living?

The relative meekness with which American home buyers are deluded by the occasional unscrupulous land salesman presents a curious contrast to the attitudes of Americans if defrauded in other lines. If a land developer scoops off an acre of priceless topsoil which took 3,500 years to form, the buyer gullibly accepts the scalped land and chalks up the loss to experience.

The prospective buyer will also want to consider carefully the character of zoning in the region. If the property is to be a small one will there be recreational lands within walking or bicycling distance—a woodland perhaps, that will stay accessible? Does the urban area have a greenbelt; a chain of public parks? The buyer of a small lot will do well to seek out that rare subdivision in which the developer has chosen, and been permitted by local zoning, to cluster the houses that land might be saved and dedicated to community use. The planned communities, now beginning to have importance, may offer sound advantages.

But the person who wants more elbow room, and some of nature's pleasures, will go farther afield. It is to him that most of this book is directed.

The Shape of the Land

A wise home buyer in the suburbs makes sure that his property is helped, rather than harmed, by the contours of the land and its vegetation. He adapts the natural topography to its best advantage. He uses every slope, tree, and terrace in preventing erosion and promoting runoff. He doesn't fight the land.

One couple in Alexandria, Virginia, was making payments on a $30,000 house in the early 1960s even though it was a pile of rubble. The house had seemed secure in 1957, but in April 1960 the saturated hillside above began to slip. Heavy snow on February 1, 1961 saturated the hill again. It slipped, leveled the couple's home, and seriously damaged those of nine neighbors.

A man who pitched his tent in a dry streambed subject to flash floods would hardly be credited with sound judgment. Yet there are numerous cases on record in which owners of expensive new suburban homes have reported flooded cellars after heavy rains. As in the case of the man in the dry streambed, more care in selecting the sites could have avoided the trouble. In the flood plain areas, zoning to restrict development will preserve stream courses and also spare possible future misery from high water.

In Lake County, Illinois, a family was nearing the end of its first winter in a new home a few blocks from the Des Plaines River. For a bargain price they had acquired a house built on alluvial soils—deposits brought down by the river. That winter when the snows melted, the Des Plaines flooded its alluvial deposit, overran the new house, and damaged it to the extent of more than $1,000. Many neighbors suffered similar damage.

The quick and easy reaction in such disasters is to blame nature and call for more levees, more state funds, and more federal funds. But this response solves nothing. The solution is not to dash ahead in a mad effort to conquer nature but to recognize the character of the natural landscape and to bend your plans to it. That means: Don't locate or buy a home on a flood plain.

The Sand Dunes

Some coasts bordering the Great Lakes, a few inland areas, and many along the seaboard are characterized by dunes; and when private ownership is involved, the individual landowner may need to undertake dune stabilization. The control of beach erosion is a subject beyond the purview of this little book.

Moving dunes can be slowed or stopped by artificial barriers, such as snow-fences, and by planting rough and tough grasses. In an emergency an emulsified asphalt and hot crude oil have been effectively used. Another remedy is the laying of a blanket of clay, four to six inches deep. This is expensive but provides soil suitable for planting. Gravel, picket fences, brush, and hay matting have all been used with varying success.

For more permanent results plant cover is necessary. The Soil Conservation Service prescribes American beachgrass as the best for dunes of the Great Lakes and for those of the Atlantic Coast above North Carolina. On inland dunes of the Great Plains, broom corn, Sudangrass, and black amber cane take hold quickly when seeded. This is usually done with the regular crop seedings.

After the dunes' advance has been brought to a halt, the grass should be followed with other plantings. On Cape Cod four species of pines took root when planted two or three years after beachgrass became established: Scotch, mugho, Austrian, and pitch pines. Southern bayberry and beach plum, both native shrubs, also were successfully transplanted in the dunes.

Great Lakes dunes have been planted with jack pine, Scotch pine, pitch pine, and common pasture grasses. Native grasses, planted into sorghum stubble in the Great Plains dunes, give the inland sands a permanent cover.

What about building on or moving back to the dunes after vegetation has stabilized them? Only with the most careful soil management. Even then there will be danger because of the continual threat of wind erosion. Catastrophe occurs quickly in the winds and waves of the coasts.

Whatever happens, repair the breaks in the vegetative cover at once, whether in the grass or trees. If you or friends insist on building, choose only the most stable dunes. Avoid those nearer shore composed of newly blown sand. Surface all access roads and trails promptly in order to hold the sand down and cause a minimum of disturbance to the ground cover.

Importance of Soil Character

"When foundations settle and crack, when new road pavements buckle and break, when septic tanks fail, or when floods drive people from their homes," says A. A. Klingebiel, of the Soil Conservation Service, "the loss . . . is not the result of an unpredictable whim of nature. It is the result of not knowing the soils on the landscape."

Most of us who live in the suburbs know little more about the soil on our property than we do about the surface of Mars. This is not as disturbing a confession of ignorance as it may sound because soils are a highly specialized field. Rachel Carson called the mystery of soil populations one of the most neglected of studies.

Lack of knowledge of one's ground may prove costly. A New York artist who moved to the suburbs discovered how much so in money, time and labor. In buying a home, he didn't realize that the developer had scooped off the topsoil. Though the site had once produced truck garden crops, there was scarcely enough soil left to grow a dandelion.

"The rain couldn't sink in, so it flooded our basement," the new owner said. "I had to buy new fill and topsoil to replace what the developer had scooped off and sold." The garage started sinking. Water had weakened the ground underneath it and the cave-in was threatening to pull the house in with it. It cost $750 to have the garage straightened and the ground underneath it shored up.

Some of his neighbors had similar experiences. One reported his patio was sinking. Several saw their game rooms turn into wading pools. The owners were baffled because their houses had been approved by building inspectors. Wherever the blame lay—and it would seem to lie heavily on the shoulders of the original owners, developers, and inspectors—even a rudimentary knowledge of soils on the part of the buyers might have convinced them that this land was unsuitable for building purposes.

Soil Formation

For most of man's existence, soil was thought of as an inert, lifeless substance. Now it is recognized that surface soil consists not only of pulverized or decomposed and dead organic matter but of living things, as does air and water. In some soils, half or more of the total volume is organic. Microscopic plants and animals engage here in the decomposition of dead vegetation and animal life to form humus. When you can make a cohesive ball from a handful of soil, it is the dark humus, essential to soil fertility, that binds the particles of soil together.

A spadeful of soil contains a seething world of its own invisible to the naked eye. Most of us pay scant attention to it, but the existence of this soil represents an intriguing mystery story going back possibly 3,600 years. That is how long it takes for five or six inches of good soil to form in temperate lands.

In this world of the soil, an endless manufacturing process is in progress. Bacteria "burn" the organic materials, producing carbon dioxide and ash. The carbon dioxide then is instrumental in activating minerals necessary as plant nutrients. Nitrogen and other nutrients in the organic material are released for plant nourishment.

Shirley Allen tells us that this plant nutrient factory in the silent, motionless soil functions at an unbelievable pace. On a hot July day, one acre of ground may be "burning carbon at the rate equivalent to 1.6 pounds of good-grade soft coal per hour, and perhaps generating as much as one horse-power of energy."

Only nature can manufacture soil and nature takes its time about it. In producing an inch of topsoil every 600 years, nature uses a variety of techniques. One source of topsoil is the subsoil—the two or three feet of earth that may be between the topsoil and solid rock. How

LIFE IN THE SOIL
(1) mite, (2) snout beetle, (3) bristle tail, (4) nematode worm, (5) false scorpion,
(6) tick. The branching structures are rootlets and mycelia of fungi.

nature makes topsoil from subsoil is an involved process. Water, frost,
chemical and root action, and air break up the subsoil rock where it is
at a favorable depth. The small particles resulting acquire soil characteristics over a long period of time in which burrowing animals serve
as mixing agents.

Soil formation is thus the result of five factors: climate, living organisms, parent rock, topography, and time. Some soils are not produced where they are found but have been picked up and borne there
by wind, streams, or glaciers.

Living With Your Land

Textures of Soil

There may be several types of soil in one suburban area. The country has tens of thousands of soil types which can be broken down by common features into about 40 great soil groups. Identifying soil groups and soil types is a task for specialists. The suburban dweller, however, can easily learn to identify the major components of his soil.

Gravel soil has the largest particles, clay the smallest. Silt and sandy soils are in between. Humus is organic in origin. Loam is a mixture of other varieties. Fine-granuled loam, rich in humus and silt, is considered the best soil because it permits the flow and storage of water, air movement, and nourishment to plant life. In the Northeast and Midwest three of the best known soils are clay, sandy soils, and humus compositions.

Clay is easy to identify. It squeezes into a smooth smear. Sand is gritty and doesn't stick together. Loamy sands stick together when moist. Sandy loam has even more cohesion. Loam has a "good feel" to it and squeezes to a very rough smear when wet. Silt loam gives a broken smear, and clay loam a smear somewhat rougher than clay.

Clay in large amounts is not receptive to water or to air. Baked by the sun, clay soil will keep out water almost as effectively as tile, which is but clay baked by man. It takes four times as long to moisten dry clay soil a foot deep as it does to moisten sandy soil—and twice as long as to wet loam a foot deep, using the same rate of sprinkler flow. Plants in such soil find it as difficult to send down roots as the gardener does to spade it. There are, from time to time, commercial products on the market which, when spaded or plowed into the soil, help make the clay manageable. One garden researcher changed a heavy clay soil into a good friable loam within four years, using seaweed (which can be obtained in both granular and liquid form) and vermiculite. For permanent improvement one must somehow achieve a proper balance by the addition of humus, sand, and fertilizers.

Soil is Solid, Soil is Porous. Percolation Tests

Soil must be able to "breathe." Good soil is well aerated, with abundant air particles. Raising the level of the land by filling in may be especially injurious. If the ground level is raised, the water table may also rise. The root systems of plants become more susceptible to disease and insects, and the plants, with roots inadequately aerated, may die. This is especially true of white oaks, beeches, tulip trees, lindens, and the conifers. If changes in the ground level of a property are made, compensatory steps should be taken to keep the root systems in approximately unchanged soil conditions.

The effects of construction on soil aeration may be more serious than direct damage to roots by careless practices. But sharing the guilt with contractors' machinery that hardens and compacts the soil are heavy farm machines such as mammoth tractors, reapers, and binders, which have left their imprint on America.

Compacted soil has other faults than being difficult to spade and unattractive to many plants. One family wondered why the septic tank kept overflowing. This was not only unsanitary in itself but it contaminated the well water. A sanitary engineer told the owner there was no solution to the problem. The soil was so heavy that the septic tank's disposal flow wasn't being absorbed. The house was condemned by health officials.

Impermeable soils always mean trouble in the suburbs if septic tanks are involved. The boom fell on one picturesque subdivision near Chicago when septic tanks began causing odoriferous patches of green in the spacious lawns. A score of $25,000 homes had been completed, of 72 scheduled for 80 attractive acres. Then health authorities investigated. Percolation tests, which measure the downward flow of water, showed that permeability of the soil was nil. The county halted construction pending installation of a sewer trunk line.

To check on the water permeability of your soils or of a home site you may consider purchasing, dig holes about root depth—two or three feet. Fill the holes with water and time its disappearance. If the water drains away in 30 minutes or an hour, you have well-drained soils and your water table is not too high. If the water hasn't disappeared in 24 hours, your property may not be favorable for the growth of most garden plants. Some communities will not issue a building permit if "perc" tests are unsatisfactory and if there is no accessible sewer line.

Fertilizers: Acidity and Balanced Mineral Content

While this is not a gardening book, we may deal briefly with the question of fertilizers since this involves conservation of the soil. While many plants are healthy in a variety of soils, others need a particularly acid or alkaline soil for best growth. The term "pH," which stands for hydrogen-ion concentration, is a quantitative measure of the degree of acidity, ranging from "extremely acid" (below 4.5 pH) to "very strongly alkaline" (9.1 or higher).

To raise the pH of a 7-inch layer of acid soil, the application of

Soil Texture	pH 4.5 to 5.5 (very strongly to strongly acidic)	pH 5.5 to 6.5 (medium to slightly acidic)
Sands and loamy sands	25 pounds	30 pounds
Sandy loams	45 pounds	55 pounds
Loams	60 pounds	85 pounds
Silt loams	80 pounds	105 pounds
Clay loams	100 pounds	120 pounds
Muck	200 pounds	225 pounds

finely ground limestone is recommended in the following amounts per 1,000 square feet for the Northern and Central States.

Garden vegetables, most lawn grasses, and common annual flowers grow best in slightly to very slightly acidic soil, as do many perennials and shrubs. Thus it is desirable to reduce the acidity (or raise the pH) in many cases to about pH 6.1 to 6.9. Some plants and trees, such as azaleas, hydrangeas, and longleaf pine, flourish in acidic soils but these are exceptions.

Equally important to productive soil is a balanced mineral content—especially of nitrogen, phosphorus, and potassium. If plants are prone to disease and spindly, an excess of nitrogen in the soil may be the reason. Big plants with many leaves but few flowers and fruits may be traced to nitrogen-rich fertilizers and lots of manure or compost. By adding phosphorus the gardener will probably get more fruit and root growth.

If the young leaves of the plant turn yellow and this condition spreads to the old leaves, it may be the result of chlorosis, an iron deficiency. Too much phosphorus and nitrogen and not enough potassium bring about such conditions. In magnesium deficiency the old leaves turn yellow first. Leaves becoming grayish or yellow and maturing too early may be traced to a nitrogen deficiency.

Erosion

Man mined the land for crops, destroyed its earth-binding cover, ripped the fields, lacerated the forests, and unfastened the soil from its God-given moorings. He handed the soil to the rains, the winds, and the rivers and saw it wash, flow, and blow away.

By 1938 a soil erosion damage chart showed 282 million acres ruined or severely damaged, including 100 million acres of cropland. Another 100 million acres of cropland had lost half of their topsoil.

In the East-Central uplands, ranging from Virginia westward through West Virginia, Tennessee, Kentucky, the southern parts of Ohio, Indiana, Illinois and Missouri to Kansas and Oklahoma, erosion is serious wherever there is sloping terrain with no cover on soils low in humus.

Loss of topsoil is not the only adverse effect. Sediment in streams, ponds, and lakes may seriously harm aquatic and wildlife ecology. Fish and plant life may die or be replaced by inferior species. Sediment in some parts of the Potomac River is nine feet thick at the bottom. The river deposits 2.5 million tons of sediment at its mouth every year.

Agriculture, and urban and highway construction are primary contributors to the streams' burden. One development in a watershed undergoing urbanization near Washington discharged 690 tons of sediment per square mile a year, compared to 146 tons for an area in the same watershed where development had not yet begun.

Soil Conservation Districts.

"The country's 3,000 soil and water conservation districts have inherited the problems and opportunities of exploding suburbia," says the Soil Conservation Service. "A common experience has been the replacement of two or three problems of individual farmers by the soil and water ailments of thousands of new homeowners."

The Soil Conservation Districts of Virginia, as one example, publishes a leaflet as a friendly welcome to builders. It informs the builder that clearing, grading, and excavation often result in erosion, siltation, and flooding; but if he will observe simple conservation practices it will be both to his advantage and that of the homeowner. Damage can be prevented and costs saved.

The Soil Conservation Service noted in its 1964 report that the use of soil surveys in urban and suburban areas continued to increase that year. In 37 areas, planning commissions and other local government or private units were sharing the cost of surveys. Soil conservation districts were conducting surveys in 364 other areas where urban expansion was taking place.

Soil Maps

A detailed soil map, as contrasted to a general soil map covering a broad area, may be made on as large a scale as four inches to the mile. Such a map is invaluable to a local government weighing an application for a suburban development. It doesn't provide enough information, however, for evaluation of an individual lot. For this, an inspection trip to the lot is necessary.

It has been a government policy for many years to prepare soil maps designed especially for certain groups such as farmers, ranchers, city planners, crop growers, and orchard growers. Of late, other groups which especially rely on the maps have been added. These groups include people concerned with septic tanks, wildlife refuges, roads, and structures.

The Soil Conservation Service suggests that all counties and other local governments utilize soils information to plan proper land use. Contractor plans should be made to conform to proper land use.

Soil maps also act as guides to the developer or architect. They are used to determine the degree of limitation for houses, for streets, or for parks. They help to avoid unstable clay soils that swell when wet and shrink when dry, causing structures built on them to shift and crack. The maps indicate where peat and muck soils exist—poor soils for foundations. They show the locations of predominantly wet soils that have severe limitations for basement foundations.

The interpretation of the soil map indicates the acidity or alkaline content of soil and tips off builders on the types of metal, cables, and concrete they should use.

Land Restoration

While the soil map's value is probably greater as a preventive to land misuse, and as a guide to proper land use, it also may be of service by indicating severely eroded lands. The owner of a building lot naturally can't expect to put into operation as many land restoration practices as a farmer does, nor on as broad a scale, but he will find some sound ideas and possibilities in the following techniques if his property is large enough to apply them.

Tillage and Furrows. Plant with the land contours rather than vertically. This will let the soil absorb more water without damaging runoff.

Vegetation. Use vegetation to prevent erosion as discussed in Chapter 4. Any kind of growth is invaluable in preventing erosion, whether the ground cover be forest, brush, sod, grain, or crops.

Terracing. "Walk" the water off the land with wide, shallow channels of gentle slope.

Diversion Ditches. Use more abrupt channels to divert water to level areas.

Gully Reclamation. Put a halt to gully erosion by damming and planting. This is discussed in Chapters 3 and 4.

Windbreaks and Shelterbelts. Rows of trees, planted at right angles to the prevailing winds, reduce wind erosion and increase soil moisture. See page 37.

Added Organic Materials. Use of fertilizers (organic), animal manure, the plowing under of crop residues, and some special crops such as clover, grasses and soybeans will help to replace nutrients lost from the soil.

Pesticide Soil Dangers. Erosion, however, is not the only soil problem in the suburbs. Soil poisoning is a persistent headache. Poisoned soils can be especially baffling if one has never used pesticides. Possibly the home site had once been a tobacco field, or a much sprayed apple orchard, or a potato field whose soils may be impregnated with persistent poisons.

In *Silent Spring* Rachel Carson reported the long-lasting characteristics of arsenic and chlorinated hydrocarbons in crop-producing soils. Toxic soils pass on their poisons to the product grown in such soils, Miss Carson reported, and the products are then consumed by humans. While this is more of an agricultural matter than it is a suburban problem, it has its application to the suburbs also—especially for the insect bomb devotee or garden pesticide fanatic who pushes the panic button at the first buzz of an insect. It takes no great amount of spraying with heptachlor, chlordane, benzene hexachloride, or aldrin to drench the soil so thoroughly that it may be years before it has weathered the effects.

Dr. Robert L. Rudd of the University of California found that "DDT, BHC, chlordane, dieldrin, and heptachlor last for long periods in soil." He reported that soils treated experimentally with 100 pounds of DDT per acre in 1947 had a residue of 28.2 pounds in 1951.

Some breakdown or conversion products have been found to be more toxic than the original residue. Aldrin, which converts to dieldrin, is one example. Several years after being treated with aldrin, soil yielded 6 to 12 times more dieldrin than aldrin. Heptachlor converts to a more toxic epoxide to such an extent that a tolerance of zero has been set for heptachlor residues in foodstuffs.

First Steps for the Individual

Faced with the possible complexity of problems and with the multiplicity of sources of help, what exactly can the individual property owner do to protect himself, for the ultimate responsibility is his. "A ground plan outdoors is as important as a floor plan inside," as one SCS expert put it.

—He can instruct his architect and his contractor to shield trees, protect their roots, and save topsoil.

—He can get technical advice from his Soil Conservation District.

—He can ask his county agent for latest recommendations from the Agricultural Experiment Station.

—He can obtain a published soil survey or field sheet of the area, consult soil technicians, and arrange with neighbors for on-site examination of their soils.

—He can learn how to use soil maps published by the Soil Conservation District and the State Agricultural Experiment Stations.

—He can plant wheat, rye, or ryegrass to hold the topsoil; can protect sloping tracts by planting or retaining vegetation.

—He can provide drainage systems when there is too much water on his land; or irrigation where there is too little, if water supplies are available.

—He can restore the soil with fertilizer, lime, and organic material necessary to keep it in good condition.

Clustering of Residences Saves Land for Recreation

The grouping of residences to save room for a playfield, a natural area, or any other community use, varies from private arrangements of a group of friends with contiguous lands, to the large-scale planning of a community, complete with shops, schools, and recreational facilities. A few land developers, unfortunately not all, provide playlands in laying out a subdivision. Some established communities are still blind to the advantages of such saved space.

As William H. Whyte notes, the cluster idea is ancient. It is simply the grouping of houses more tightly together, allowing more land to be used for common greens and squares. "Cluster" is similar in some respects to the village green designs of early New England towns in which use of the village green and the peripheral area outside the village was shared.

In modern times a wealthy Englishman named William Whiteley pursued a variation of the idea. In 1910, at the cost of a million pounds, Whiteley created Whiteley Village to blend the graces of country and urban living. He formed the center of the community in the shape of a hexagon. The village then radiated outward through 225 wooded, rolling acres. Whiteley has stores, a bowling green, pavilion, library and other services. It still accommodates 100 men and 260 women.

In Florida, a comparable plan was proposed in 1950. It called for 500 or more living units around a community center and would help to accommodate the suburbanites of a city of 50,000. About a fifth of the community would live in apartment houses, the rest in one-story units on landscaped lawns. Stores and shops would be available in the heart of the village. Rural minded people would live on the outer edge where they could cultivate fruit orchards and crop gardens.

Whether the cluster concept will help man attain better equilibrium has not been proved. Cluster proponents contend that it will. The buyer selects a house on a smaller lot than usual, or possibly an expensive town house as part of a row house development. In either case the property is part of a neatly designed development. Wooded streams and walkways take the place of concrete culverts. A community woodland brings nature near at hand and, with open area for recreation, provides a wholesome atmosphere and refreshing scenery. Reston, Virginia, is an application of cluster development to a planned community, and Columbia, Maryland, promises to carry the principle yet further.

One semi-rural community, Village Green at Hillsborough, New Jersey, devoted 35 acres to three clusters of houses, leaving the remaining 40 acres open. The builder saved money on water and sewerage installations because he could use existing trunk lines and didn't have to dig wells or install septic tanks. He also saved because he could construct three more houses than under the conventional plan. Land development costs dropped from $6,500 to $5,000 per unit because less grading and fewer roadways were needed.

Needless to say, this book will be of little help to the dweller in a planned cluster community which provides all services and leaves little for the individual to do.

Greenbelts—to Halt Sprawl

The British were pioneers in protecting the countryside around some of their cities with "greenbelts." These were intervals of open land where relatively little building was allowed. A strand of wooded farm land around London today is a good example of a greenbelt. And one result is high land values for residential areas in or adjoining the belt.

The greenbelt idea may prove fertile ground for American planners. To be sure there have been some greenbelt communities in the United

States—Greenbelt, Maryland, and one at Cincinnati, Ohio, for example —but this British type of greenbelt consisting of land only, could well supplant the ugly no-man's land that surrounds so many American cities. This is the belief of G. P. Wibberley, a University of London land economist well acquainted with American urbanization. Professor Wibberley sees the greenbelt as a check on residential sprawl. A wooded or farming strip would replace the auto graveyards, the collapsing shacks, neon honkytonks, and derelict lots that garland our cities in ugly disarray. Wibberley calls these fringe areas "rural deserts."

"Man," comments conservationist Dr. Paul B. Sears, "is clearly the beneficiary of a very special environment which has been a great while in the making. . . Its value can be threatened by disruption no less than by depletion. . . . Humanity should strive toward a condition of equilibrium with its environment."

This is the challenge that faces suburbia.

Great blue heron

Muskrat

3. Water, On and Under Your Land

When you buy a suburban home, you acquire not only the land but the water on and under the land (springs sometimes excluded in New England). Yet many people scarcely give the underground water a second thought.

If a pond, a lakeshore, or a brook is involved, you may sign your purchase agreement with a smile. The water represents a valuable and visible property asset. But what about the invisible water, the underground water table? In our contaminated environment of today, the nature, quality, and extent of the water table are of more importance than ever. The underground water, if you are not connected with a public water system, is your personal supply. The plant life, lawns, and general appearance of your property are also dependent on a favorable water table.

Thus, the amount, quality, and depth of water under your plot may prove more important than you first realize. Drought, contamination of aquifers by industrial and unsanitary seepage, pesticides, and detergents are certain to place strain on water supplies as to quantity and quality. If you are restricted in watering your lawn and plants from a public water supply, your only salvation will be access to ground resources. If you have a septic tank, compacted soil, or erosion by waters flooding down from higher elevations, it will be wise to know a little about your water table.

Water Tables: High and Low

As defined by the Department of Agriculture, the water table is "the upper limit of the part of the soil or underlying rock material that is wholly saturated with water." Thus, the water table simply represents the highest point where accumulated water in the ground has leveled off. Under average conditions, the best water table level to have in the Northeast and Midwest is about 30 to 48 inches below the surface of the ground.

Occasionally what appears to be a water table may be only a "perched water table," and is easily polluted. This is the top level of a shallow accumulation of ground water that was unable to seep down to the true water table or to a water-bearing stratum. A well tapping a perched water table might run dry quickly whereas a water-bearing stratum might last for centuries.

Tree stands affect the height of the water table, acting as pumps to soak up the water and pass it off into the air. This is the transpiration step of the hydrologic cycle, the series of processes which make up the life story of water. Water is evaporated into the atmosphere from the oceans and lakes, condenses, falls, and soaks into the ground. Here it is absorbed by plants and passed off in transpiration, or it replenishes the water table, or it reaches streams and flows to the sea or lakes where the cycle begins anew.

If the water table is too high, the septic tank effluent may be within the water table. With the first hard rain, the effluent then may merge

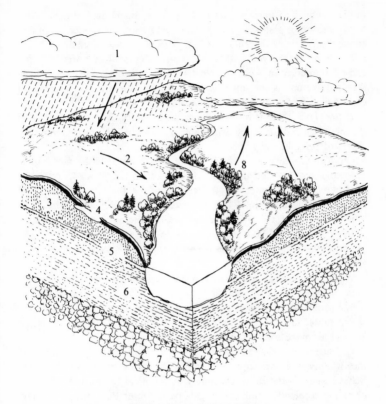

THE CYCLE OF WATER

Rain from the clouds (1) will run off (2), in part, while some seeps into the soil to the "zone of percolation" (3). Where this zone bleeds to the surface it may form a spring (4). More water, however, will find its way down to the water table (5), below which is a zone of saturation (6), often sealed below by bedrock (7) or heavy clay. Water evaporates from the surface, and from trees is released by transpiration (8); the water vapor rising to form new clouds.

with the undrained water covering the saturated ground. The resulting stench is bad enough but the health risks are worse.

If the water table is excessively high and continues so, action must be taken. Otherwise, flood conditions may weaken home foundations as the runoff carries away terraces and hillsides. If the soil happens to be of clay composition, the runoff velocity will be increased.

Another adverse effect of an excessively high water table is the long-range damage to garden plants. It isn't so much the cold that kills hardy wintering plants as it is waterlogging from the winter's rain and snow. Contrary to the belief of many people, wet, saturated soils are not inviting to the roots of most plants. Roots must "breathe" and can't if immersed in water. In most soils plant roots receive the oxygen they require unless the soil is fully saturated. Roots must also give off carbon dioxide and this process is hampered by water.

If the water table is too low, there is difficulty in keeping trees and shrubs, grass and garden growing, and in preventing the sun from baking and hardening the soil.

On a community scale the lowering of the water table may cripple the water supply—and the community also. In the Santa Cruz Valley of Arizona, when water use tripled—from 420,000 acre feet in 1941 to 1,250,000 acre feet in 1949—the water table fell 50 feet. In the Antelope Valley of California artesian wells seemingly inexhaustible in 1910 with a flow of 900 gallons a minute had ceased to flow by 1920. Other wells were tapped, but by 1950 they were falling three feet a year.

Water scarcity is not confined to arid regions, however. The Department of Agriculture warned, as long ago as 1955, that serious groundwater problems existed in the eastern half of the United States. The water table had fallen near many industrial centers, and as far as 30 miles or more around some cities.

In December 1964 the village of Fonda, New York, a few miles up the Mohawk River from the industrial cities of Amsterdam and Schenectady, found its water supply at a critical level after months of drought. Ironically, millions of gallons of water flow past the village daily in the polluted Mohawk River. "Our reservoirs are running dry, our water table has sunk out of sight," Fonda's mayor told *The New York Times*. Two farm ponds were hooked up to the community water main. A factory's 50,000 gallons a day were cut off, and the plant used the Mohawk's waters instead. School was closed for two days but opened when milk tank trucks brought in water for the school mains.

When a water table falls, a community's health, income, and general welfare may fall with it. One factor goes up however—the fire insurance rate. A dry hydrant may be disastrous not only to the owner of the burning building but to his fellow insurance buyers as well.

The Department of Agriculture has proposed two solutions to falling water tables: Severely reducing the rate of pumping from wells, or substantially increasing the rate at which the ground water is replenished by artificial recharge with excess surface water.

To maintain a water supply at the desired level, there are techniques of raising or lowering the water table much as one lowers or raises the level of a swimming pool. With forest stands which once regulated the water table largely gone, irrigation, usually subirrigation (or underground replenishment), is used to regulate the water table. From 1949 to 1954 irrigation in a 31-state area of the East, Midwest, and South increased 70 percent. Subirrigation, designed to hold the water table at 12 to 30 inches below the surface, injects water directly into the ground. Obviously a good supply of surface water is needed, as well as smooth, nearly level ground. It is also advisable to have a permeable soil below the surface soil and a relatively impervious layer underneath the water table to restrict excessive percolation. East Central States in which subirrigation has been used to control water tables are Michigan, Indiana, Minnesota, Wisconsin and Ohio. This is not a matter for the owner of a small property, but a community or government affair.

Drainage and Erosion

If your land is more than a small suburban lot, check drainage needs. Try to learn if drainage outlets are adequate, if excess water can be removed from the soils, where the water comes from, how much must be drained, and what type of drainage system to use. For a drainage project, it is advisable to: (1) review contour maps, aerial photographs, engineering reports, land use history, and other data; (2) make a personal reconnaissance and a study of ground configuration; (3) make a soil survey from borings; (4) make a water table survey from observation wells that reveal fluctuations of the water table and percolation barriers. Advice on such matters is available from your local office of the Soil Conservation Service.

Hilly ground is poor for drainage purposes. The Soil Conservation Service warns against drainage projects for slopes of more than three percent. Ground from level to a two percent slope is considered excellent. Erosion has been a persistent spectre in the East-Central uplands where slow permeability of soils results in excessive runoff.

Marshes and Swamps

Although marshes and swamps may be of lasting value to the property or community around them, such sites are usually avoided for home sites. The mistaken belief that the only good swamp is a drained swamp is discouragingly prevalent, a reflection, perhaps, of our ignorance and failure to educate along lines of ecological principles.

In our zeal to prepare more land for "development" we have drained lands that should have been left as they were. Swamps and bogs have been drained; estuaries have been channeled, their lowlands covered by dredgings and other land fill. We need not read the word "progress" in such activities. Swamps, marshes, and bogs covering 62 million acres represent the habitat of hundreds of species of animal life. The country might be richer today if at least some of these wetlands had been left in their original state, to keep a touch of nature about us and to preserve our wildfowl, mink, muskrats, and other marsh wildlife. Many hunters agree with non-hunting conservationists on this question.

Encouragement of certain types of plants in a swamp, marsh or pond is likely to prove rewarding in the wildlife they attract. Many waterfowl require such stands for food, nesting, and cover. Ditches, dug to drain off excessive water in swamps and marshes, may retain water during dry spells and thus sustain wildlife that would abandon a dry marsh. Cattail marshes remain stable without much attention unless hit by an exceptionally severe drought. If the water level is maintained for an 18- to 30-inch depth, nesting in offshore sites is likely to be encouraged since the water acts as protection against raccoons and predators.

Many common plants of coastal marshes are the frequent food of waterfowl: pondweeds, wild celery, pigeon grass, smartweeds, watershield, water lilies, the spikesedge or spikerush, naiads, some rushes of the marshes such as needlegrass rush, and some bulrushes. Ducks like arrowhead and sawgrass seeds though the plants usually grow too dense for good duck feeding habitat.

On inland marshes with waters as high as two feet, muskrats will respond to cattails, arrowheads, burreeds, bulrushes, and sweetflag.

Streams and Valleys

Streams and valleys have charm, but they also may present problems of flooding, erosion, and pollution.

The quality of the water is important. Most of our river systems and many lakes—including the Great Lakes, except for Lake Superior—are badly polluted. Even if we should soon succeed in cleaning up our waterways, other serious water problems remain.

The average small stream, however, is not of interest to suburbanites primarily for the water it might supply. A stream is, or should be, appreciated or of concern because of its drainage value, its erosion hazard, its relation to the water table, its aesthetic and recreational values.

The Soil Conservation Service provides assistance through the local Soil Conservation Districts to anyone wishing to improve a watercourse, construct a pond, or accentuate the values of a marsh or swamp. Local or state public health officials will check your waters for pollution, a precaution which should not be overlooked.

Gullies

Study the channels that water follows across your undisturbed site. They should be left intact as often as possible, including their natural cover of trees and grass.

The Soil Conservation Service advises lining small seasonal water channels with grass in converting them from gullies to runoff courses. Small gullies—those less than eight feet deep—can be converted into non-destructive drainage channels if the drainage area is no more than

A FIRST STEP IN GULLY RESTORATION
Runoff will be slowed by brush-choked fences. Planting, and the construction of diversion ditches should follow.

about 50 acres. If the runoff channel is shaped and planted with appropriate grasses, the resulting vegetated waterway should carry the runoff without erosion when the flow is reasonably paced and of moderate duration.

A broad, flat channel allowing a flow about 6 to 18 inches deep at 3 to 6 feet a second is recommended. These gully waterways, the Service says, should stand dry for part of the year since continual moisture would kill the vegetation. To provide protection of this type to ravines and stream courses, as well as to acquire recreation areas in private developments, some communities allow the developers reduced lot sizes in exchange for the desired acreage.

Artesian Waters

If you are lucky enough to have an artesian, or flowing, well on your property, don't credit it to your water table. Artesian waters are not free ground waters such as those of the water table. They

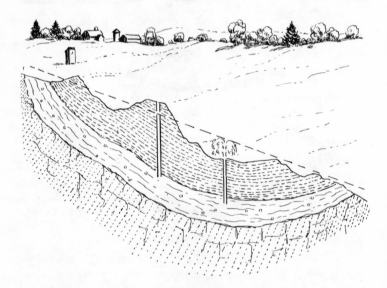

THE ARTESIAN STORY

Surface water, moving downhill through porous soils or rock sandwiched between impervious layers, may at points lower than the source waters be tapped to produce a flowing well. Such a well will not necessarily be unpolluted, as suggested by the sketch.

are imprisoned in a porous layer between two impervious layers, and depend on a water source which must be higher in elevation and which may be quite distant. The resulting gravitational pressure produces a steady flow of water, a "flowing well." Artesian waters are an extra dividend to the suburbanite or farmer establishing his own storage pond or reservoir.

Ponds

Most of the suburban and farm ponds familiar to passing motorists, however, are of the impounded type created by damming a seasonal drainage channel or stream. An earthen dam, commonly 10 to 30 feet high, is used to create an artificial lake. Such lakes may hold up to 300 acre-feet of water; that is to say, surface area times average depth.

The pond's value does not end with stabilizing the water table nor even as an emergency source of water in dry periods. It serves as a reliable reservoir for fire fighting, attracts wildlife, may make a fish pond, fosters vegetative growth, and adds beauty to the area. Every foot of clean water pays off recreational dividends—in swimming, fishing, boating, and ice skating. A pond is a jewel in the birdwatcher's lexicon for the variety, extent, and importance of the habitats and species it accommodates. An impoundment serves to check erosion and helps to hide erosion scars.

Artificial lakes are popular in suburban areas. Costs of erecting them by stream impoundment may run, as estimated by the Department of Agriculture, from $700 to $36,000. The cost depends, among other things, on the height and length of the dam, size of the impoundment area, cost of spillway design and chutes, leakage and seepage problems, and soil textures encountered.

Ponds may also be created by dredging swamplands, as is often done by real estate developers who thus create additional higher priced home sites.

Estuaries

The importance of estuaries as units in the biological and economic picture has recently become an area of national concern, and not only because of marine areas ruined by industrial activity, marine development, or land fill. It is the estuaries that are the nurseries for much of the coastal waters' wealth of fish, shellfish, and birds. If your home is in an area where alteration of a natural estuary is threatened, you should act quickly to force mature consideration of such action.

True improvement of shore areas is best left up to shore experts—

Living With Your Land

and that includes those who know shore wildlife. One of the best waterfowl breeding areas in the vicinity of New York City was barely saved
from real estate developers in 1963–65. The marsh-like stretches off
Hempstead, L.I., have been used every summer for centuries by waterfowl but the shallow waters looked inviting for "development." Filled
in, the marshes would provide lucrative acres of waterfront property.
Fortunately, Hempstead conservationists, with the guidance of the National Audubon Society and supported by the U.S. Fish and Wildlife
Service and the New York Conservation Commission, were able to save
the endangered waters—and waterfowl—from invasion.

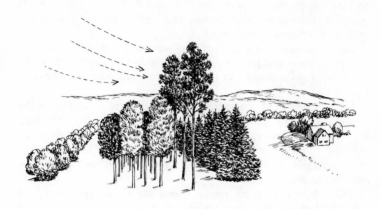

WINDBREAK
A band of trees and shrubs, planted on the windward side of a house will protect it from blowing snow and chilling and eroding winds. When they are placed, as here, with an outermost row of shrubs, blowing snow will be trapped behind the first of the barricades.

4. Vegetation, High and Low

A homeowner visited his newly purchased suburban lot the day before a contractor was to break ground for a new house. The property appeared only vaguely familiar. It looked like the wake of a scorched earth policy. The bulldozers had scalped the ground so thoroughly that the soil lay glaring in the sunlight, as bare as a bowling alley.

The homeowner winced. He had closed the purchase with a $5,000 down payment and a substantial mortgage. But he winced for another reason. He had mentioned to the real estate people that he would like to have the young Australian pine tree and some pitch pine saplings spared as the nucleus of his landscaping design. The message apparently never reached the contractor.

The suburbanite (this author) had learned a lesson. Fortunately, the trees, shrubs, and grass that he planted grew rapidly in an especially favorable, high moisture climate. Yet he mourned the loss of the Australian pine.

The existence there of any trees was possibly a minor miracle as the acreage had been scarified some 10 years earlier for use as a melon field (the trees were new growth). There were indeed "melons" there—in the form of choice real estate lots. But the lots would have been even more desirable if the original trees, shrubs, plants, and wildflowers had been spared.

At the front door of my present home, like a silent sentinel, stands an old black spruce. To a concerned friend this towering ship's mast is a threat to family safety in the event of lightning or a wind storm. To us, the spruce seems more like a strayed wanderer from the northland—sprung perhaps from a seed dropped by a migrating bird generations ago.

Our friend's advice is sound, however. The time to fell or trim big trees whose size and branches could damage a house, or whose roots could block a sewer line is before trouble starts. To wait until a branch or the tree itself falls might prove costly and dangerous. In the case of a new home, the contractor should take care of this problem before he starts building.

Value of Vegetation

You may have what seems an adequate plant inventory on your land—grass, trees, ornamental shrubs, and a flower bed. But there are other values of which this chapter will treat. One may wish to plant to provide better nesting sites and better food resources for birds and other wildlife. Autumn color could perhaps be improved. You might take pleasure in establishing a wildflower garden.

Most of us in the suburbs desire trees, shrubs, and grass to enhance the appearance of our property. Only later do we realize, perhaps after some study, that the values of vegetation may be more significant and far-reaching than the decorative role. For example:

1. Vegetation prevents soil erosion by wind and water, as discussed in Chapter 2.

2. Vegetation acts as a strainer or cleanser of that part of the rain-

fall that finds its way into the soil. Without this cleaning action, particles of soil adhere to raindrops and clog up air passageways in the soil. (One scientist substituted turbid water for clear water in a laboratory test and found that some soils lost 75 percent of their absorptive power after eight hours of dirty water infiltration.)

3. Trees help to regulate the water table (see Chapter 3).

4. Trees and shrubbery help to cool the property in the summer with their shade and moisture retention, and "warm" it in the cold months by acting as windbreaks.

5. Trees absorb noise. Their foliage reduces traffic hum and thus makes areas along highways livable.

6. Trees and shrubs attract a variety of birds that may afford pleasure and interest in their action and song.

7. A balanced vegetation is important to the ecological relationships of all living things on your land.

Sponging up the Rainfall

A study by the American Water Works Association found forests the most effective plant cover. Of 13 vegetal covers evaluated, forest duff (and permanent pasture sod) proved easily the most effective in slowing down runoff, cushioning the erosive force of water, and promoting infiltration. Their erosion rates of 2 or 3 percent compared with 10 percent for alfalfa land, 60 percent for wheat fallow, 90 percent for orchards, and 100 percent erosion rate for row crops and fallow.

Another study, this one made in the field at Bethany, Missouri, on an 8 percent slope, showed alfalfa to be the most effective erosion foe. Compared to grass, corn, rotation of crops, and fallow soil, alfalfa fields lost the least topsoil and retained the most water over a four-year period. This was in a region with a 40-inch annual rainfall. Fallow soil lost more than 100 tons of soil per acre, corn about 60 tons. Grass lost only 660 *pounds* per acre and alfalfa 560 pounds. Grass lost only about 8 percent of its rainfall, alfalfa about 4 percent, but corn and fallow soil nearly 30 percent.

The success of plant cover in controlling runoff is a minor achievement compared to the way plant cover softens and absorbs rainfall. Raindrops the size of peas fall as fast as 30 feet a second compared to the three-feet-a-second horizontal velocity of runoff from a gentle slope. Comparing a sheet of rain with a runoff flow is like comparing Niagara with gentle Afton.

A two-inch, one-hour rain produces an energy equivalent of 250 horsepower per acre—possibly 100,000 times the kinetic energy of runoff from the same storm. Plant life is contending here with a force that produces a dead weight of 100 tons when only an inch deep over one acre.

Plant cover not only cushions the destructive splash process of a raindrop, absorbing its energy, but interrupts the travel of the splashes. A study of over-grazed pastures in Tennessee showed that in some rains 700 pounds of splashed-up soil are caught per ton of forage vegetation. The amount of splashed soil caught does not include the undoubtedly large amounts washed off the vegetation by the rain.

Tree Selection for the Small Estate

Any wise home buyer wants trees with his purchase—the more, the better. Trees, especially venerable shade and evergreen trees of stately distinction, add character to suburban property. They link us with the dim past and the future. Some scholars see a connection between man's misuse of the land and the quality or permanence of civilizations. A century ago, George Perkins Marsh, the brilliant American minister to Italy under President Lincoln, blamed the collapse of Mediterranean civilization largely on deforestation and other land misuse.

Whether you plant trees for ornamental reasons, shade, windbreaks, shelterbelts, or to control gullies and other erosion, it is advisable to consult local authority. Your state agricultural experiment station and county extension agents know what varieties are best suited for your locality.

For shade and ornamental purposes, the American elm, maples, and oaks probably have had the strongest hold on our affections in this country.

The American elm for three centuries has been a most favored tree by reason of its graceful shape and rapid growth. If you plant elms, however, you run the risk of having them killed by the Dutch elm disease. No means of preventing the disease had been found as of 1967. An expensive method of inoculating trees against the bark beetles that carry the fatal fungus was still in the experimental stage at this time. Pennsylvania State University has maintained 400 of its campus elms by prompt elimination of sick and dead limbs harboring the beetles, by pruning, and by careful spraying when the beetles start roaming in the spring. The fog-type spray of 25 percent DDT in a zylene base, mixed with equal parts of water, was applied on windless nights to lessen drift from the target site.

The fungus kills most European elms as well as the American elm. Chinese and Asiatic elms and a variety of European elm, the Christine Buisman, are less susceptible to the fungus than the American elm but lack its beauty of form. Elm seedlings may be obtained from Elms Unlimited (see Appendix A) at low cost, This organization supports research and seeks to keep pace with Dutch elm disease losses by planting seedlings.

Excessive planting of any one species of tree is unwise. An insect infestation or disease can reach disastrous proportions in an uninterrupted stand or boulevard of trees of a single species. Our heavy planting of American elms in so many communities has made it easier for Dutch elm disease to wipe them out. Elms should be interspersed with other trees, if used at all.

An affliction has also hit the beloved sugar maple. In the East, salt was blamed for extensive tree kills in 1965. Some 500 dying maples along a major highway which had been salted to melt ice and snow led to a chemical analysis of the leaves and twigs. The tests showed excessive amounts of sodium in the leaves and twigs of trees close to the highway and within its drainage area. Parasitic fungi are reported to be responsible for some of the die-off. Additional study will be necessary to determine if the ailment is indeed the result of sodium poisoning or whether it is endemic. An excellent booklet on maple tree problems is available from the New York State College of Forestry. (See references in Appendix B.)

There are other good maples—the red, Norway, and sycamore maples; and the brittle but colorful silver maple. Small Japanese maples, featuring reddish leaves in summer, are especially popular.

Oaks are a solid asset to any property. Most oaks attract birds, squirrels, and other wildlife. The best known and most successfully planted oaks in the North include the white, red, pin, and black, sometimes called yellow *(Quercus velutina)* oaks. Pin oaks like a wet and acid soil. The acorns of the handsome red oak, which has red blossoms in spring and wine-red leaves in fall, are too bitter for most wildlife.

Oaks, too, have their troubles. Where water tables have dropped, the trees do not remain healthy and bark boring beetles may proliferate and girdle the tree, killing it. Oak wilt is attacking many trees, and is less understood than the elm disease. When leaves turn brown out of season, its presence is to be suspected. A remedy has not yet been found. The yellowing of leaves in an oak, known as chlorosis, is a sign of iron deficiency, and may be treated by a tree specialist through feeding iron to the root system.

Tulip trees, beech, linden, poplars, and white ash are good looking. Mulberry trees are popular with birds but messy in fruiting season. Flowering dogwood, redbud, catalpa, horse chestnut, and shadbush are spectacular in their flowering season.

Plant evergreens for variety, for winter beauty, screening, or for bird attraction. The northern white cedar or arbor vitae is one of the most widely planted and hardy evergreens, excellent for hedges and screening. Of the spruces, the Colorado blue and Norway are popular for their symmetry and color. The white pine is a good provider to red squirrels and some birds, but is subject to several diseases. The aromatic balsam fir and eastern hemlock also are handsome and good seed producers.

One of the hardiest trees for dry, gravelly, or very sandy soil is the so-called Chinese tree-of-heaven, ailanthus. It may shoot up six to ten feet in a season, to provide good shade, but its crushed leaves or bark give off a disagreeable odor. The white or "cat" spruce has a similar problem. The ancient ginkgo, also Asiatic, is a handsome tree tolerant of air pollution, but the female trees bear evil smelling fruit.

In selecting tree species, consider too those species whose fruits have value as wildlife food. The several hickories, though slow growing, provide squirrel food. Walnuts and butternuts are useful to both animals and man. In the southern fringe of the territory considered, paw paw and persimmon provide interesting fruit. The Osage orange, once popular as a hedge plant because it makes dense cattle-proof fences, has lost its popularity on farms because it narrows the land available for planting, but it is still popular with birds that find in its dense tangle fine nest sites. The green orange-sized fruits have a very pleasant odor, and in the house fit into table arrangements with both appearance and scent. The dense yellow wood makes excellent cutting material for the craftsman.

Trees as Windbreaks

According to tests made by the Kansas State Board of Agriculture, a 35-foot-high windbreak puts the brakes on a 30-mile-per-hour wind so effectively that it slows the wind to 21 miles per hour even 100 feet from the planting. The real effectiveness of trees, however, is on their leeward side. Here the wind has been stopped almost in its tracks. Within 100 feet of the trees, the wind has been slowed to a maximum of 8 mph, at 200 feet to 10 mph, and at 300 feet to 14 mph. Thus the windbreak pulls the teeth of a biting wind that could be a disastrous erosive force. Slowed down to 8 to 14 mph, the wind is much less effective at whipping up miniature dust storms and carrying top soil into the next county, nor can the wind now dry up the soil as fully. The trees nip dust aborning.

A windbreak offers some protection even 1,500 feet away. This could mean the difference between a spring freeze and fresh vegetables. In

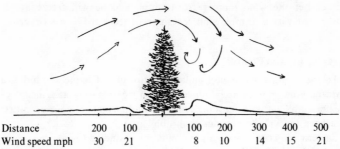

Distance	200	100		100	200	300	400	500
Wind speed mph	30	21		8	10	14	15	21

This is the pattern of wind eddies that drop driven snow behind a windbreak of evergeens.

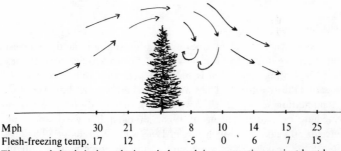

Mph	30	21		8	10	14	15	25
Flesh-freezing temp.	17	12		-5	0	6	7	15

The same shelterbelt, by reducing wind speed, is a protection against heat loss to man or dwelling. A 30-mile-an-hour wind 200 feet to the windward of a shelterbelt will freeze a person's exposed hands or face at 17° F. At the same distance on the lee side, the wind would be reduced to 10 miles an hour, and one would not freeze in the same length of time until the temperature reached zero degrees.

WIND EDDIES

the winter, a windbreak can mean the difference between intolerable cold in a suburban yard and a pleasantly brisk day. If oriented to deflect summer breezes towards the house, planting may also reduce the cost of air conditioning. Know your seasonal winds before screen planting.

The wind's faculty for turning a $30°$ overcast day into a bitterly cold, ear-freezing, sub-zero-like torment is familiar to most of us, for wind has the effect of cooling the body sharply.

In a 2-mph wind, an inactive man can withstand cold up to $40°$ below zero, at least for a few minutes, before his exposed surfaces freeze. Let the wind increase to 10 mph and he will freeze at 2° below zero; with a 30-mph wind, freezing will occur at 17° above zero.

Trees for Erosion Control

To the treatment of small gullies mentioned in Chapters 2 and 3, a word may be appropriately added here on tree planting as a means of greater stabilization of eroding land. It is important, of course, to first arrest erosion with herbaceous or shrubby growth.

Eastern red cedar, Scotch pine, pitch pine, and red pine are recommended for the Northeast and Middle Atlantic regions. Virginia and shortleaf pine are also suitable Middle Atlantic choices. In the Northern Great Plains, use red pine, eastern red cedar, willow, elm, or poplar.

Tree Plantations

It is practicable to plant trees on non-forested idle land for investment. Planting costs may run only about $10 to $20 per acre. If there is a $10 planting cost, returns on good sites may run from 4 to 9.5 percent on the investment. There are regional differences, however.

A plantation set out in 1957 would be nearly ready for selective intermediate pulpwood cutting in 1968, although full yield would not come for 30 years. A 15-inch tree in 1963 was worth about $9 as logs, $10 as a utility pole, $5 as wood pulp—and how much more as a living monument?

The plantation is not limited to long term production. Improvement cutting from time to time may yield three to eight cords of firewood per acre, some fence posts, and possibly some lumber for home use.

What trees make the best private forests for profit? For drier northern areas, the white pine, red pine, and Norway spruce are good. In slightly moist northern regions, pines are recommended for warm areas and black locusts for cool areas. For moist sites, consider red oak, black locust, white oak, butternut, and black walnut. (The nut trees grow slowly, but their woods have high value.) The white ash and maple are advisable in better drained bottom soils. For flood bottom soils or soils having high water tables, the cottonwood is recommended.

Professional advice on how to use the family forest or plantation to best advantage is available from federal, state, and local public agencies; from forest industry sources and from consultant foresters. Your state forester probably can recommend a good private consultant. State and federal extension forestry help is available through your county agent.

For a variety of cost-sharing services, consult the nearest Agricultural Stabilization and Conservation Service; for low-interest loans see the Farmers' Home Administration. The forest industries can offer competent professional help.

The Tree Farm Program, launched in 1941, had 25,000 certified tree farms by 1962. It has come under some criticism of late on the ground that it does not give sufficient consideration to ecology. Underbrush and competing plant life often are eradicated in an effort to make a "clean" tree farm and the result may be inimical to wildlife interests. Single-species tree stands are considered a mistake as an invading disease may wipe out one's full investment.

The Woodlot

If you have purchased a farm in an area that has been largely divested of its forest growth there may still be a "woodlot," a forest remnant which previous generations had kept as a source of stove wood or of logs; a retreat for livestock in the summer heat, and a place to turn pigs loose for the autumn downfall of acorns and nuts. Perhaps it was a sugar-bush, and could, with work on your part, be one again.

If the area is large enough it might be used as a revenue producer of logs. Selective cutting of a woodlot does not rule out the presence of wildlife. It will encourage the introduction of some species of birds and mammals which would have shunned the more mature habitat.

If a landowner has decided to stress a timber-producing woodlot, herbicides can help attain that goal. Some mixed stands of conifer-hardwoods may suppress growth of a white pine understory unless the hardwoods are thinned—a task which herbicides can do. A white pine three feet in diameter that has had the opportunity to grow tall and straight may be worth as much as $250 compared to a "no value" rating for a crooked or rotted white pine of the same size, age, and board feet. Some hardwood logs suitable for veneer cutting may be worth several hundred dollars. Almost any tree represents cash, if it is not defective, if it is large enough for processing, and if there is a sawmill nearby. In planning a cutting operation, it is well to seek the services of a professional forester. A mill operator will not necessarily have the landowner's interests at heart as much as his own.

Great trees, however, aren't always best evaluated in dollars and cents. If the owner is willing, his woodlot may contribute recreational and educational values to his neighbors and may be a treasure to the entire community.

Trees and Lightning

Tall and isolated trees attract lightning much as does a lightning rod. An average bolt produces about a billion volts and high voltage ionizes or breaks down the air around the tree. Thus, when the current inside the tree becomes strong enough the ionized air facilitates the current's formation of a lightning arc around the bark. This is the process that strips trees of their bark.

Old and valued trees may be given a measure of protection by the installation of lightning conductor cables from their summit to the ground.

Avoid isolated trees during an electrical storm. Obviously, anyone standing near the tree becomes a likely conductor to which the lightning may jump, or he may be the target of a bolt attracted by the tree. A rocky pinnacle is also a high risk in an electrical storm.

If a person is struck by lightning and stops breathing, try mouth-to-mouth resuscitation.

Dead Trees Still Useful

All trees, like animals, have limited lives. Some, such as the poplars, are short-lived, other species live for centuries. A dead tree is not necessarily one that was diseased; it may but have lived out its life span or succumbed to lowering of the water table or to root injury. Such trees might well be left to follow the course of nature unless they overhang a roadway or are potentially a source of danger to a dwelling.

A dead tree is a good place for woodpeckers to feed and to excavate nests. When one of these holes is vacated by the woodpecker's brood it becomes available for others: perhaps a flying squirrel, a chickadee, wren, or nuthatch. Trees with large hollows will shelter fox squirrels, raccoons, opossums, and some owls. Beneath loose bark bats and some harmless snakes may find sleeping quarters. Before you remove a dead tree weigh its values in relation to your own interests.

Shrubs

The importance of shrubbery is obvious, whether for screening the house foundation or the neighbor, for adding color to the place, or providing bird food. There is a wide choice of good species. Some are well suited to the formal garden, others, such as the hazelnuts, are better fitted to fence rows or woodland edges. For a selection suited to your area you will find help in some references cited, and from your nurseryman. See, too, the section of this book on attracting birds.

The Wildflower Garden

There are so many legal restrictions on the moving of wild plants as to discourage most people from developing a wildflower garden unless his own property is already blessed with species he can transplant or enjoy in their natural habitat. No plants can legally be removed from any property without the permission of the owner. This is true whether the property is private or public, and applies even if a bulldozer is about to destroy the native vegetation to prepare the land for building.

Even with the permission of the owner, no plants may be moved without written evidence of prior inspection by authorities from the Department of Agriculture, according to what is called the Nursery Law, which is designed to prevent the spread of plant diseases. Furthermore, a number of states have enacted laws to protect certain species of rare plants. Anyone who wishes to acquire wild plants should acquaint himself with the provisions of these laws, information which may usually be obtained from his state conservation or natural resources department.

There remains the possibility of buying what would be considered wild plants from a nursery, and several specialize in supplying this type of plant. But even here, the buyer must be able to produce a bill of sale proving he bought the plant from a nursery that in turn can produce its proof of inspection.

If all these requirements can be met, the next consideration must be the matter of soil and shade. Few native wildflowers will long survive a transplant without thorough preparation of a good bed. If it is to encompass a woodland selection, bring soil from the woods into the place you choose, spade it in, cover it with leaf mold, and let it age. A half-rotted log will help to establish a variety of conditions.

Bloodroot, spring beauty, trillium, jack-in-the-pulpit, hepatica, and phlox are among species transplanting well. Violets are attractive but tend to take over the space. Ferns of several species may do very well, and the maidenhair, royal, ostrich, interrupted, and Christmas ferns are to be particularly recommended.

Poisonous Plants

The Public Health Service has estimated that 12,000 children are poisoned each year by plants, and that surely does not include poison ivy nor the rash developed from contact with nettles. Peach tree leaves contain hydrocyanic acid, a poison. Rhubarb leaves contain oxalic acid, which can cause kidney damage. Many other common garden plants are poisonous in flower, stem, leaf, berry, seed, or root; among them,

Nightshade (*Solanum*)

larkspur, lily of the valley, sweet pea, monkshood, autumn crocus, and bleeding heart. One would not eliminate such plants from the garden, but one should learn to recognize them to protect the younger members of the family.

One species might be especially mentioned because it is attractive, abundant, and very poisonous if ingested. This is the nightshade, a close relative of the tomato. All parts of it are poison. Though its violet, purple, or white flowers are attractive, as are its bright red berries, if there are children about it is prudent to destroy the plant.

The rash and blisters caused by poison ivy and its close relatives, poison oak and poison sumac, are unpleasant and can be quite discommoding. Should a child eat one of the small white fruits or a leaf it could be a very serious matter.

Poison ivy grows as a shrub, vine, or sub-shrub. Over most of our area it may be found both as a shrub and as a climber, but in the northern fringe (north of the 44th parallel) the tree climbing habit is not found. The species flourishes on flood plains, sand dunes, and bottomlands, but is seldom encountered in oak-hickory or oak-pine woodlands. It is characteristically three-leaved (rarely five- or seven-leaved). Learn to distinguish poison ivy from woodbine (Virginia creeper), which is five-leaved, young box elder, and hoptree.

The poison oak is similar in habit to the ivy but differs in leaf shape (see illustration). Poison sumac grows at the edges of swamps where it is a tall shrub, often occurring in dense stands. Though its poison is even more virulent than that of its relatives, fewer people are affected because few wander into the swamps where it occurs. The leaves in autumn are strikingly handsome and add great beauty to the lowlands.

The ivy plant's toxic effects are probably more prevalent in late summer. By this time it is fairly well grown and insects may have bitten into the leaf, allowing the poison to escape from its resin canals. Now merely by brushing the leaf one may incur poisoning. Many cases of poisoning come from contact with shoes, clothing, garden tools, or pets that have had contact with the plant.

Shortly after exposure, use of strong soap, such as Fels Naphtha, has proven helpful in avoiding a rash. But at this time there seems to be no universally effective medication for ivy poisoning. In light cases a bland compress, such as aluminum acetate (USP) solution, 1 part to 20 parts of water, is helpful. Such treatment should be followed by calomine lotion to dry up the dermatitis and ease the discomfort. The effectiveness may be enhanced by immersing the poisoned area in very hot water for a few minutes before the lotion is applied. In severe cases cortisone derivatives may help but these drugs should be administered only by a physician.

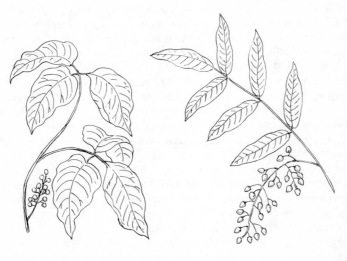

Poison ivy   Poison sumac

To get rid of poison ivy, weed killer herbicides (such as 2,4-D) are effective but they must be used over a two- or three-year period until there are no more viable seeds or roots. If plants are removed by hand, both the plant and gloves should be placed in a bag for trash removers. Burning is dangerous for the poisoning droplets travel on dust and ash particles and can be severely damaging if they reach the skin or lungs.

Mushrooms and Toadstools

A toadstool, in common parlance, is but a mushroom you shouldn't eat; a mushroom but a toadstool you may. There are, in fact, many fine fungi commonly eaten which, because they are not umbrella-shaped, should not be called toadstools. Such are the puffballs, morels, and truffles (the latter, alas, almost unknown in our land).

No matter how great your appreciation of mushrooms as food you must never eat wild-picked specimens unless you have become thoroughly acquainted with them—and the alternate possibilities. Gathering and eating the wrong species, no matter how safe they look, could be the death of you. Almost every late summer brings a rash of mushroom casualties and hospital stomach pumps are worked overtime. Yet thousands of careful people find great pleasure in their harvest and the utilization of good species.

If your nearby university offers an extension course in mushroom identification you might widen your interests and knowledge by enrolling. For the names of reliable mushroom guide books see the reference pages. Remember though that no book identifies all species that you are likely to encounter, and remember too that individuals vary greatly in their tolerance of mushrooms. Never overdo a good thing and on first exposure be especially cautious. Any mushrooms taken in large quantity can make almost anyone ill. Try them on the cat, if you wish, but remember that the cat's tolerance may not be yours.

A person who has eaten a death's cup mushroom *(Amanita phalloides* or *A. verna)* faces almost certain extinction for the symptoms of poisoning do not appear for 10 to 24 hours after ingestion and by then the damage is done. Two poisons are at work, one destroying nerve and gland tissue, the other, like rattlesnake venom, separating blood corpuscles from the blood serum. Another species, the fly amanita *(A. muscaria)*, paralyzes the nerves that control the heart action. Atropine injections are sometimes helpful to a victim of this species. Take no chances. Rush the patient (and some of the mushroom if available) to the hospital emergency room.

Of Fences

"Good fences make good neighbors," as they say in New England. In another sense than is meant, good fences *bring* good neighbors from a naturalist's point of view. Such a border could be a split-rail fence, with shrubs and weeds in the angles and a tangle of vines along the line. These fences make a home for game birds, a highway for squirrels, and a refuge for many sorts of wildlife. Unfortunately there are few railsplitters left and few places where one can buy rails ready made. Perhaps the most practical way to acquire them is to buy remnants of an old rail fence. Because rail fences are wasteful of space some farmers will not tolerate them and might welcome an opportunity to replace them.

If a rail fence is not available, a wire fence flanked by brush and weeds will do almost as well. Hedges of Osage orange or of multiflora rose also provide good wildlife shelter, though they have drawbacks in relation to agricultural production.

Grass Burning

The widespread spring practice of burning old grass in field and meadow, does encourage the growth of new grass and cuts down on some weed growth. The dangers, however, may outweigh the advantages. Fire exposes the soil to erosion and encourages the growth of even less desirable plants. Repeated burnings sometimes are followed by an invasion of highly inflammable cheatgrass. Grass fires also can reduce the soil to ash or sterility.

Above all, grass burning is a dangerous undertaking because such fires often get out of control and burn woodlots and buildings. Burning should never be undertaken except on a calm day, with ample personnel and equipment to keep the fire under control, and with prior permission of your local fire department.

In burning, avoid areas with poison ivy. Droplets of its poison travel on smoke particles and can produce a severe rash or lung trouble.

Herbicides

In recent years an unnamed genie residing in a herbicide bottle has played the role of assistant gardener to many a suburbanite. Herbicides have been instrumental in the creation of a plant life environment adapted to the owner's needs.

While pesticides poison the environment and wildlife, most herbicides offer little danger. Many herbicides are selective; that is, they are not fatal to narrow-leaved herbs such as grasses. In selecting a herbicide, however, check the contents. Chlordane and arsenic in a pre-emergent crabgrass killer proved to be also a songbird killer.

Once the homeowner has decided what type of vegetation effect he wants for his property, he can proceed to attain it, if climatic and soil conditions are right. Some part of the land, if in untouched heavy thicket, should be saved for wildlife; but in other areas, for scenic purposes one may wish to thin the plant growth. Undesired small trees, vines, briers, and brambles will yield to herbicides.

Herbicides are proving of value also in thinning over-stocked woodlots to permit growth of better quality trees. This applies to private and community woodlots and even to the small wooded stands occupying a corner of the one- or two-acre suburban site. Some will prefer to let the woods grow the way nature sees fit.

Some ponds and lakes may be improved for fishing by control of both submerged and emergent vegetation; or by dredging, an expensive operation. The algae (pond scums), of which there are some 1,500 species in this area, can be controlled by several chemicals, copper sulfate being the safest. It may be scattered by hand from a boat, or in lump form placed in a gunny sack which is then towed behind a boat over the affected area. If not overdone it will not kill fish. Other presently available algicides are dangerous to use because for a short time at least they are poisonous to domestic and wild animals. Conservation departments are usually in a position to guide one to commercial lake cleaners.

Woodchuck

5. *Neighbors in Furs*

The mammals on your land may be fun to watch but some will prove nuisances in your garden, your attic, or your stream bank. This little volume cannot identify them all for you but will point out areas with which you may be concerned and name those species that are well worth encouraging. You may already be a bird watcher and have a bird feeder and birdhouses. Give some thought to putting up shelters for tree nesting mammals, and establishing feeding stations for both nocturnal and diurnal furry visitors. By flashlight or floodlight they can add new interests to country living.

Some animals are more prevalent in the Eastern States today than they were in Thoreau's time, the 1840s and 1850s. He was so saddened by the extirpation of some species around Concord that he said spring was "like an imperfect copy of a poem. My ancestors have torn out many of the finest pages." Changes in land use have brought about some recovery.

Deer. The population of the whitetail deer is up in many areas, and they survive at the edges of some of our largest cities. In summer they may hide out in wooded areas but in winter come into orchards and gardens where they may be a nuisance. You may lose some valuable plantings to them but perhaps the pleasure of watching them will be worth some loss. It would take an eight-foot fence to keep them out, or a dog tied in the yard. In winter when natural foods are most scarce it may be necessary to put strong chicken wire around your most vulnerable yews or rhododendrons. Don't take the law into your own hands. Some states provide indemnity for losses to orchards.

Mothballs hung in cheesecloth sacks from the branches of an orchard tree, or cones made from four-by-six-inch squares of tar paper placed on branches will effectively keep deer from feeding there.

Deer may be winter fed with pellets (commercially available) or with "apple pumice," the residue of cider pressing, generally freely available from mills. The artificial feeding of deer in winter is frowned upon by many game management people for it tends to develop a larger deer population than the vegetation can naturally support. Left to themselves they will roam the orchards feeding on unharvested apples. Putting out salt blocks for deer may attract them to your premises but do not do this without consulting your game warden. A salt lick attracts hunters too.

It is estimated that each year 50,000 whitetails are killed in traffic accidents in the states covered by this book. New York's take in 1958 was estimated at 24,000. Pennsylvania reported 12,153 in 1963; Michigan, 4,146 deer-car accidents in 1962. Annual nationwide car damage from deer is estimated at $15 million, or $150 per car involved. While most of these accidents may occur in the more remote areas, many do happen in the environs of suburbs.

How can you avoid hitting a deer? Keep alert in deer country for the bright glow of deer eyes in your headlights and slow down if you see it. If a deer does dash to the other side of the road, watch for one or two more to follow. Let them get off the road before you start. Suppose you do collide with a deer; what do you do? *Traffic Safety* magazine says to get the animal off the pavement quickly so it won't wreck cars. Place the deer on the road shoulder.

State laws vary as to whether the driver may keep the deer his car has killed accidentally. The Michigan law permits the driver to keep deer accidentally killed. In Wisconsin, local game wardens have the responsibility of picking up the car-slain deer. It is unwise to put a car-killed deer in your car. There is considerable deer poaching and hijacking, and the conservation officer may think your tale of an accident is an unlikely story indeed.

At least nine states have been testing deer accident preventive systems based on a successful Dutch technique. Small mirrors, about

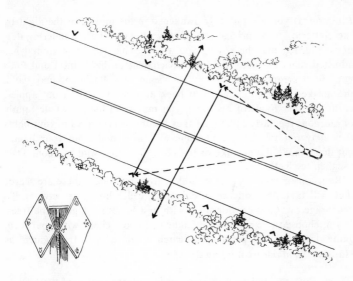

three inches wide, are placed three feet above the ground on metal posts set along the road at about 25-foot intervals. The mirrors are angled at 45° from the highway edge to reflect the glare of oncoming headlights in a deer's eyes, causing the deer to "freeze" as when beamed with a searchlight. Favorable results had been reported by some states, but a 1967 report based on Michigan studies concluded that there was no significant difference in incidence of collisions in mirrored or unmirrored roadways.

Car damage in an accident involving an animal should be paid under the comprehensive or collision coverage of one's automobile insurance.

Living With Your Land

In 1962 the National Automobile Underwriters Association ruled in effect that animals are flying or falling objects, covered by a comprehensive insurance clause.

However, most homeowners are not protected against animal damage to their property. Homeowners Insurance Form 5 will provide protection against damage caused by wild animals. Most hospitalization and medical policies cover animal-caused injuries.

Bear. You won't find a bear in the average suburb, but this big lumbering connoisseur of bee's nest honey now roams fairly close to some of the larger cities in the East. Bears are exciting to watch, and usually not dangerous, but nobody in his right mind will get close enough to a black bear, cub or adult, to find out.

Raccoon. If you are suddenly awakened in the middle of the night by the clattering of a garbage can, it may of course be a wandering dog, but a raccoon may be paying you a visit. This attractive animal has adjusted remarkably to man's encroachment on his habitat and finds your food scraps to his liking. The beam of a flashlight may catch the masked robber looking right back at you. If you put out apples, corn, or other foods of his liking you may soon have a whole family of raccoons regularly calling. As they become accustomed to your lights they may not run away and some will take food from your hands, but don't make the mistake of trying to pick up a wild raccoon. They use their teeth effectively.

Raccoons commonly nest in hollow trees but where these are scarce they will take up residence in chimneys, cellar holes, or culverts. To encourage raccoons provide them with nest boxes set high in the trees. If you choose to be rid of an offending raccoon, check with your local game laws and if permissible catch it in a live trap (such as Havahart) and release it far away.

Foxes. Both red and gray foxes occur in suburban areas of the Eastern States though the gray, essentially a southern fox and a tree climber, is rare in many parts of its former range. The foxes are not averse to catching ground nesting birds but their service to the landowner in feeding largely on mice, rabbits, and insects makes them good neighbors. The actions of a fox, whether leaping at grasshoppers or baffling the hounds, are a joyful sight and fortunate is the suburbanite who has one nearby.

Skunks. These white-striped black animals thrive in settled areas where houses are not crowded closely together. They are sensed much

1. The woodlot path is a fine escape from town and the well-tended garden.

2. A gully head. Erosion was stopped by diversion ditches and by tree planting 18 years before the photograph was made.

3. Serious erosion accompanying construction can be largely eliminated by well-planned grading or early planting.

4. This windbreak of multiflora roses and evergreens, already effective, will stop drifting snow and wind erosion in its lee.

5. A multiflora hedge, planted to a contour, provides shelter for wildlife. It needs neither wire nor fence posts.

6. The fence line devoid of cover is good for the farmer, but offers nothing of interest to one interested in nature's crops.

7. A wire fence flanked by native shrubs gives birds and mammals good cover.

8. A rail fence, its reentrant angles grown to elderberry, blackberry, cherry, and weeds, gives nesting cover to quail and a safe wildlife corridor.

9. Floodplains in the dry season seem choice building sites. Remedy for the owners of these homes is beyond their individual control.

10. Soil conditions will be considered by the careful buyer of a home site. Here there is soil slippage on a hillside.

11. A stream kept clean can provide good sport.

12. The pond, rich in value for nature study. Who would drain it?

13. A ditch in a marsh provides homes to muskrats, ducks, and many other water dwellers.

14. The raccoon—woodsman and suburbanite.

15. The skunk. He also enjoys good lawns where he can dig for beetle grubs.

16. Following animal tracks lets one learn much of the maker's wanderings, and feeding and social habits.

17. A baby cottontail is cute, but won't tame well. If handled when it is in the nest it may be deserted.

18. The barn swallow, too, likes country life and will help rid your grounds of flying insects.

19. The bobwhite in winter lives in coveys, rarely taking to wing unless disturbed.

20. The woods in winter. Brush piles here have furnished shelter for rabbits and small birds.

21. The woods in spring. Their beauty is fragile: a trillium if picked
will not appear next season, since the leaves are needed to create
food for future growth.

22. Spring burning. It gives the grass an early start, but destroys much organic matter, pollutes the air, and all too often gets out of hand.

more often than they are seen. In food habits skunks are omnivorous and beneficial in their consumption of young mice and the large beetle larvae that infest many lawns. A skunk's search for these grubs is often evidenced by small scattered pits in the sod. A little foot work will close the pits. Skunks will stay away if the grubs are killed by chlordane, though this insecticide also kills useful soil animals and its general use is not recommended. Skunks also eat grasshoppers, crickets, beetles, and cutworms. Thus, these mammals may be valuable allies to a farmer, unless they raid his hen house or bee hive.

A skunk's odor is disagreeable, though the scent is not evident unless the animal has been recently annoyed. Skunks have roamed around my homes in Wisconsin, New York, and Florida without any unpleasant incident. If skunks do visit your premises regularly it is well to keep the dog indoors at night, the time these animals are active.

Skunks sometimes take up residence under houses or porches and it is well to have tight foundations. If a skunk does make your home its home, place bait well away from the den, then close the entry; but be careful that there are no young skunks in the nest. Mothballs poured into a den should cause the skunks to move. Shooting can be disastrous. Live trapping is likely to be a less troublesome means of getting rid of your guest. The trapped animal may be moved elsewhere.

The scent of a skunk lies in the oily secretion of two glands under the tail, and is one of the most powerful odors known. The weapon is used, however, only under great provocation. The animal raises its tail, aims the twin jets at its enemy while looking back over its shoulder, and, to a distance of as much as 12 feet, can be pretty accurate. If the spray hits the eyes it is said to be quite painful but not productive of lasting harmful effects. Ample application of water will alleviate the pain, but not the odor.

There are several schools of thought on getting rid of the odor of skunk-sprayed objects. Tomato juice (good on dogs), gasoline, and Roman Cleanser have been recommended. The cleanser is a bleach. Earlier generations buried sprayed clothing in damp earth until the odor disappeared. A more modern method is to place the clothing on an activated charcoal filter in the path of a strong fan. The absorbtive surface of the charcoal is said to absorb the odor.

Skunk watching is fun, for this clownish animal is frequently amusing. Edwin Way Teale, the naturalist, puts out food for skunks and then watches them amble into his yard. Skunks don't take readily to a pecking order; they do a great deal of shoving, bumping, and hip-shaking in crowding ahead to the food handout. Another observer at such a feeding station has watched the skunks push aside raccoons and an opossum that shared the table. Skunks are reluctant to waste their ammunition. Thornton W. Burgess, another nature writer, once picked up a skunk whose head was caught in a bottle, gently broke the bottle on a stone, and so freed the skunk, which made no attempt to spray.

Because they are principal carriers of rabies it is unwise to make pets of wild skunks. In Michigan, where over 30 rabies cases were reported in 1963, it is unlawful to have a skunk deodorized if it was caught in the wild.

Weasels and Mink. Weasels are important harvesters of the mouse crop and wild mink will help to keep down the population of muskrats. There is little that one can do to encourage the presence of weasels and mink beyond providing the proper habitat. But one can discourage the trapping of these animals on his land.

Dogs and Cats. If you have a dog or a cat this section is no place to seek advice. If, however, you are not a dog or cat owner and you are bothered by some other person's pets or by feral animals, the following suggestions are appropriate.

Packs of wild dogs, sometimes interbred with coyotes (the coydogs), plague deer herds in some of our Eastern States. Such dogs should be shot on sight. Your neighbor's dog is another matter and short of fencing there is little you can do other than to practice throwing stones or to become proficient with sling shot or BB gun. A steel trap of suitable size with its jaws wrapped in multiple layers of cloth to prevent injury to an animal foot, may teach a dog that its presence is not required but will not create new friends for you.

Stray cats may help keep down your mouse and chipmunk populations but will also enjoy hunting the birds. A good treatment for a stray cat is to catch it in a wire box trap baited with fish or other favored cat foods and then teach it a lesson with a garden hose. If you are sure that the cat is homeless, offer it as a gift as a laboratory specimen, or dispose of it painlessly.

Dr. Paul Fluck says that the average cat kills 50 birds a year. Each person will have to determine how he will cope with this problem. One suburbanite tolerates cats for two visits. On each visit he pins a note on the cat saying that the cat's third visit will be its last. Another resident said he ties a "dead ripe" substance around the cat's neck and lets the cat go home. We keep a few rocks on hand. Rarely do we hit a fleeing cat but it is good exercise and apparently jars the cat's confidence.

Opossums. Although opossums are essentially southern animals, their range has extended northward and now includes southern Ontario. Adult opossums at the northern limits, however, often show loss of their ear tips and tail tip, the result of winter freezing.

Opossums are grayish animals with a naked scaly tail, naked ears, and a somewhat pig-like face. The adults are about the size of a house cat but shorter legged. Although they are excellent climbers, for which the grasping hind feet and prehensile tail fit them, they nonetheless often occupy dens in the ground. Slow moving, they may be readily overtaken, whereupon they commonly feign death. Opossums are little changed from their ancestors of 115 million years ago. Despite an apparent low intelligence, they are remarkably successful in adapting to changing situations. As in their second cousins, the kangaroos, the young are brought forth and travel to the maternal pouch in an extremely larval state. There they remain firmly attached to a teat until their eyes are open and they are capable of moving about to their mother's back, or independently.

Opossums are economically beneficial in their consumption of mice, grasshoppers, and beetles. They are omnivorous, however, and the gardener may resent their raids on corn, grapes, apples, or berries. Opossums also occasionally empty a bird's nest or invade a chicken roost.

Though readily caught, opossums make poor and uninteresting pets. Despite their formidable teeth they are harmless and inoffensive. At a feeding station, however, they may be interesting to watch for they eat deliberately, unhurried by mere humans or a curious small dog. Feeding them things of your choice may serve to keep them away from the garden.

Moles. The presence of moles is most evident in the raised roofs of their tunnels in lawns, but in their subterranean sightless existence they also burrow in woodlands and fields. One species, the star-nosed mole, is found in low wetlands and is a capable swimmer. The eastern common mole and the hairy-tailed mole have broad, strong hand-like paws fitted close to their bodies, which equip them for digging their extensive tunnels.

Moles derive most of their nourishment from earthworms and grubs and it is their ceaseless search for food that leads them to your lawn. Complaints that moles follow rows of garden plants and destroy them are usually unfounded; the damage is most likely attributable to rats and pine mice that use mole tunnels. Bear in mind the fact that aeration of the soil and destruction of grubs are useful acts of mole activity.

If you eliminate the moles' food by application of chlordane or other

Deer mouse

House mouse

Shrew

Norway rat

Mole

killers of soil animals you will rid your place of moles but this wide spectrum poisoning will also disrupt a biological system and may have undesirable consequences. The use of poisoned baits is generally ineffective though placing mothballs in the tunnels at 8- to 10-foot intervals is reported to be an effective deterrent. A campaign limited to the use of mole traps will do the least to upset nature's balance. A government pamphlet (U.S.D.I. Conservation Bulletin 16) gives good advice on mole control.

Shrews. The shrews, of which there are several species in the area with which we are concerned, are small, sharp-nosed, with short velvety fur and minute eyes. All are dwellers in the leaf carpet of woodlands or in grasslands and make or use shallow underground tunnels. Few people see them unless they have fallen into cellar holes, yet they may be numerous. They are fast-moving, voracious feeders upon seeds (the short-tailed shrew is an occasional visitor to bird-feeding stations), insects, snails, worms, and frogs. Although posing no threat to humans, they are possessed of a cobra-like venom with which they paralyze their larger prey. The shrews in our economy are to be rated beneficial.

Mice and Rats. You will be most fortunate if you have left the house mouse (an import from the Old World) behind in the city, yet other mice will be your neighbors. The house mouse is foul-smelling and a spoiler of food as is the even less desirable neighbor and camp-follower, the rat. All methods of getting rid of them are fair. Because Old World mice and rats are destructive of food and property as well as carriers of disease their presence must not be tolerated.

House mice are easily trapped in either live traps or spring traps. Cheese is all right as bait but corn meal or peanut butter will do as well. Rats are more cautious and soon learn to avoid traps so that poisoning is a better way to be rid of them, but be careful where the poison is placed and what kind you employ. Warfarin is generally accepted as being the safest since it has little or no toxic effect on man or domestic animals. Prepared poison baits, such as RAM (for rats and mice) and D-Con, may be left in open dishes in attics or unattended dwellings. Should first efforts to get rid of these rodents be unsuccessful it would be well to obtain one or more of the inexpensive pamphlets on rats listed in Appendix B. These give adequate information on recognizing signs of rats, provide sound advice on rat proofing the premises, and advise on techniques for exterminating the pests. The use of poison requires care and mature judgment.

Wild mice are another matter. Most apt to be encountered in one's home is the dainty and clean white-footed or deer mouse. In a wood-land cabin these mice may become quite at home with you and at dusk appear to watch you and perhaps attract your attention by drumming with their forefeet. They can make amusing pets. But do not forget that these are rodents and they can and will make nests in your linen or pillows if they have a chance.

In open grassy areas, particularly in lowlands, a common mouse will be the meadow mouse or vole. It is short legged, short tailed, and shaggy. These mice rarely invade houses but may destroy ornamental plantings and make nuisances of themselves in orchards. Commercial rodent repellents may be applied to your ornamental shrubs, if you recognize signs of the bark being eaten, though the danger is greatest under the snow and may not be detected before a thaw. The repellents should remain effective for three or four months. To avoid girdling keep long grass away from tree trunks and don't mulch your plants until after the first freeze for such cover affords protection to the mice. Place metal screening about three-quarters of the way around the trunk to a height of about eight inches, or as high as the snow may drift.

A close relative of the meadow mouse is the pine mouse, but this animal is largely subterranean in habits, and may cause annoyance by gnawing roots, especially of conifers, or by following underground a row of garden plantings.

Squirrels. What squirrels live on your land? In the area with which this book deals there are many possibilities. Among the tree-dwelling species there are the flying squirrels, red, fox, and gray squirrels. Ground-dwelling species include the chipmunk, the 13-lined ground squirrel (sometimes miscalled "gopher"), and the woodchuck, which is dealt with here under its own heading. Each may interest the land-owner one way or another but almost anything with gnawing teeth will prove a nuisance at times.

Tree squirrels may be encouraged to stay around if one leaves trees with nest cavities nearby or provides nesting boxes in the trees. These should be similar to birdhouses but with the entrance on what would be the side of a birdhouse to make access easier from the trunk. Entry holes must be appropriately larger and the inside walls should be rough. For specific recommendations see the new edition of E. J. Sawyer's booklet on bird and animal house construction.

Squirrels will be encouraged if they are fed. They may be provided with coarser food than that given small birds: corn on the cob or an occasional animal bone. Their feeding shelf should be separate from a bird feeding shelf, for squirrels like sunflower seeds in quantity. Feeding squirrels by hand is to be discouraged for there is always the possibility of a bite transmitting rabies. The chance is minuscule but the risk might as well be avoided.

Squirrels that find a way into attics or walls present problems. As soon as such a situation is discovered find out where they are coming in. When you are sure that the squirrels are outside, plug the hole. They have been known to chew insulation from wiring and the hazard here is obvious. Red squirrels often get into summer camps or cottages and cause damage to mattresses, blankets, and upholstered furniture, a fault which they share with the white-footed mice. Blankets and linens should be stored in trunks or chests and not in cardboard boxes. But the best protection lies in having an animal-proof house, its chimney equipped with a closeable damper or a screened top. You can make a building virtually squirrel-proof by fitting flexible sheet aluminum between the roof overhang and the building wall and nailing the metal snugly.

Red squirrels are unpopular with many bird watchers for their occasional raids on birds' nests, a habit not unknown to other squirrels. Man, too, is omnivorous.

Flying squirrels are nocturnal and hence seldom seen, but they may be baited into feeding trays where they can be watched in the early evening. They commonly nest in the cavities of old apple trees where they compete with screech owls, starlings, house sparrows, and bluebirds. Nature writer Ann Rockefeller has described one way of observing these gliding mammals whose "flights" may take them as far as 228 feet. She devised a baited terrarium or feeding box that projected through the wall of her bedroom, and equipped the box with one-way mirror glass, making the interior visible from her room.

Flying squirrels taken young may be readily tamed and make excellent pets. If caged during the day, their time of sleep, they can be given freedom of the house while the occupants are watching. Their cage should be moderately spacious and be equipped with an exercise wheel.

Ground squirrels in the Eastern States present no problem. They construct tunnels in the soil of grassy areas but unless a foolish dog tries to dig one out the hole will remain small and inconspicuous.

Chipmunks are at times a nuisance as when they take up residence in a flower garden, for they will eat the bulbs of some crocuses and occasionally destroy other plantings. You might try feeding them something else; if that fails you may need to choose between chipmunks and their chosen flower. If they can reach your bird feeder, they will keep it empty until the time of their winter sleep.

Woodchucks. Woodchucks, or groundhogs, are most abundant in open fields but as their name suggests they also occur in woodlands and are capable of tree climbing. They will not be encountered in densely populated areas but often take up residence under or alongside rural houses. When they become a garden pest a .22 may be the best answer, though a frequently tended live trap baited with apple or carrot can prove effective. The animals may be killed in their burrows with poison gases but this has attendant dangers. Safest, where the site admits, is piping automobile exhaust fumes into the burrow for 10 to 15 minutes and sealing the hole. Do this only in warm weather, however, when the chucks are active. At other seasons their burrows may be shared by useful animals.

A cornered woodchuck is a formidable antagonist to boot or dog, so keep a safe distance.

Porcupines. Porcupines don't come into the suburbs but are familiar to many dwellers in the New England States by the evidence of girdled and dying evergreens. Tree girdling is itself enough to make the porcupine unpopular but when one of these animals gains access to a camp and chews an axe handle or a canoe paddle where perspiration has made the taste salty, or when aluminum cooking pans are destroyed, a porky arouses real resentment.

Porcupines are known to chew even rubber tires, perhaps because road salt is on them. Some woodsmen decoy porcupines away from camp by soaking a log with brine.

Copper naphthenate or pentachlorophenol ("Penta") will repel porcupines if painted on the gnawable surfaces. The copper mixture will turn wood a greenish color unless a weak solution is used. Both substances are harmful to trees and shrubs, but so are porcupines which might have to be removed if not repelled by chemicals. If a wooden live trap is used in the process of removal, it must be lined with sheet metal or stout hardware cloth if it is to confine the animal for long.

If your dog comes in contact with a porkie's tail, the spines, which are barbed, will have to be removed with pliers. Porkies cannot "shoot" their quills.

Rabbits and Hares. The only time many suburbanites know that they have rabbits as neighbors is after the snow arrives. Then the familiar footprints and marblelike scats are noticeable. The cottontail is the most familiar species in the Northeast and Midwest. It differs from the hares in its shorter ears and legs, smaller feet, year-round brown coat;

and in the female's use of a brood nest, a small cavity scooped out of the earth and lined with her own fur. In this the young spend a few days until their eyes open and they are strong enough to move about. If such a nest is discovered leave it strictly alone. The mother will not return to the nest if her young have been handled.

The true hares do not construct a nest. Their young are born with eyes open and within a short time are capable of moving about. The only native hare in the Eastern States is the varying (because it grows a white coat in winter) or snowshoe (because its large hind feet are even broader in winter). The hare is a denizen of the northern country and here will occasionally be seen about dwellings. The European hare, which may weigh as much as 13 pounds, has become established in much of the East and the Great Lakes area. It is not commonly encountered in well settled areas. It has occasioned a good bit of damage to shrubbery and young orchards.

Hares and rabbits both patronize gardens and young orchards. Screen collars to protect fruit trees from girdling should extend above the animals' reach in heavy snows and should either be left unfastened where the ends meet, to allow for tree growth, or should be set out an inch from the trunk for that purpose. Hail screening ("hardware cloth") in half inch or smaller weave will protect plants from both mice and rabbits though metal fly screening alone is adequate for mice.

Bats. These small flying animals are among the earth's most remarkable creatures. Their ability to locate flying insects or to detect obstacles in the course of their nocturnal flight by bouncing sound waves from the object before them, and their trick of flying with their young attached are but two of many aspects in bat biology that make them incomparably intriguing.

Bats may startle people by their swift, erratic flight, but none of our northern bats, except a rabid one, would by choice alight on a human. There are a few known cases of rabid bats in the United States, and any bat that would light on a person should be captured and taken, with cautious handling, to the nearest health service. There are no vampire bats in the north. Our species are all insectivorous and by this designation are considered helpful. Experiments in providing bat shelters as a means of increasing their local population and decreasing insect populations have been without success.

Some northern species are solitary, others colonial. They may take up residence in an attic or behind shutters, and because the excreta below their roosts can become offensive there are occasions when they are not welcome. Naphthalene flakes in large amounts placed below their roosts may drive them away. Some brush-on repellents are effective where bats shelter behind shutters.

Muskrats. If you have a body of water with soft edges and emergent vegetation, the muskrats may build their domed houses of swamp plants there. Then leave them alone for the animals are a pleasant sight, and if unmolested show little fear. Their houses sometimes serve as egg laying sites for turtles and nesting platforms for water birds. If they tunnel into lawns at a pond's edge, or into an earthen dam, their removal may be called for.

Traps and Trapping. There are circumstances when it is desirable to remove animals from one's property. Poison, except for rats and perhaps moles and mice, should never be used. Use of guns on some animals can be justified but only in the hands of a good marksman and then only when local laws permit. Traps are the best answer for most animals. Lethal traps are most humane but there are no generally available types for larger mammals. Steel traps are cruel and in some areas are justly under legal control—as is their use against many species in every state. Live traps have a great deal of merit for the reason that the catch is uninjured and may be released in some more suitable area or, if the animal caught is not that intended, may be released on the spot. Live traps must be regularly attended, however, at least once in early morning and again in early evening, otherwise the animal may break out or suffer from exposure. A live trap put out overnight must contain some nest material, lest the animal die of exposure. The best generally available live traps for medium sized animals are those made by the Havahart Co. of Ossining, New York 10562. They are available through mail order houses and some local stores.

Of Animal Transmitted Disease. Avoid close contact with any wild mammal, dead or alive. The uncertainty of a wild animal's reactions may bring an unwelcome bite or scratch; or one of its parasites may move to you, not to stay but long enough to bite. Rabies and tularemia ("rabbit disease") are the principal risks. Rocky Mountain spotted fever occurs in the Eastern States too. It is borne by wood ticks which are to be carefully avoided.

Rabies has been transmitted by skunks, foxes, bats, raccoons, opossums, squirrels, woodchucks, muskrats, and other mammals. Even cattle and horses may carry it. Stay well away from an animal appearing sluggish or wounded, or which is acting abnormally. The important thing to remember is that if anyone is bitten by an animal that animal must be captured or killed. If captured, it will be held under observation by the authorities for at least 14 days. If killed, the carcass must be turned over to the health authorities for examination. Anti-rabies vaccine must be promptly administered if the animal proves rabid or if the animal has not been captured or killed. It is unpleasant to have the series of vaccine shots but the alternative is possible death.

Tularemia may be contracted through a bite, scratch, or the bite of an infected animal's external parasites. Handling a wild rabbit that you may have found or shot or purchased in a market is unwise.

There is no reason, however, for hysteria or even alarm about the small risks of contracting disease from wild animals, just caution and common sense. Fewer people die of rabies than of insect stings. In 1964 there was but one human death from rabies in this country though some 30,000 were given anti-rabies vaccine. The danger from domestic animals is of course far greater than from wild ones because of the greater exposure.

Food chain

6. Of Bird Life

The increasing interest of Americans in bird life reflects our growing maturity as a people and the increase of our leisure time. The earliest colonists had all they could do to survive, and wresting an existence from the wilderness took more than a 35-hour week. Today, however, many families watch birds as a pastime with all the teamwork of a plane-spotter crew. Nature is nothing new to the suburbs but, as suburban life increases, more people are new to nature.

Men who grew up in rural New York State may discover that the red-headed woodpecker that they saw as boys is now relatively rare. But the presence of cardinals in goodly numbers more than makes up for it. If bluebirds are noticeably scarcer, the equally colorful blue jays seem more numerous. Species they had never seen as boys are now fairly common—the tufted titmouse and white-breasted nuthatch, for example.

Spring and fall bring migration flights and the excitement of watching Canada geese fly overhead, honking steadily. Some suburban dwellers form moonlight bird watching sessions and use telescopes to watch migrating species fly past, silhouetted against the moon. Wild geese and ducks are among those visible. Experienced bird followers can identify the calls or "chips" of the migrating flocks of smaller birds as they pass overhead—some species by day, some by night.

Identification

Suburbanites who like birds around their houses think along the same lines as Thomas Jefferson, who kept a list of more than 100 species that he could identify and who had a pet mockingbird that followed him around the White House. Unlike Jefferson, however, who had to rely on such cumbersome and expensive reference works as Mark Catesby's *Natural History of Carolina, Florida and the Bahama Islands* (1731), we have a choice today of several bird guides and scores of other bird books. Most states have standard works on the birds found within their boundaries. Local areas have checklists. The guides of Roger Tory Peterson and Richard H. Pough are invaluable for either house reference or field trips. In addition to the guide books, recordings of bird songs are available. (See Appendix B.) Recordings not only reinforce visual identification but satisfy the curiosity of all of us who wonder "what bird sings that song?" Albums produced by the Laboratory of Ornithology at Cornell University are designed to accompany Peterson's field guides to birds.

This method is pursued even further in *Song and Garden Birds of North America* and *Water, Prey, and Game Birds of North America*, published by the National Geographic Society. Each of these books has a long-playing record album, each record marked so that the phonograph needle may be placed at the song of the species desired. Most songbirds in the North sing only during their nesting and breeding seasons and as a means of marking out territory. (The Carolina wren and mockingbird are exceptions.) A bird's singing period also depends largely on the latitude and weather conditions.

Birdhouses. Birdhouse construction is booming. Some factory and do-it-yourself sources are pressed to keep the supply in pace with the demand. People seem to want birdhouses as badly as the birds do. Here is a gratifying and constructive trend. Obviously the clearing of a million

Table of Birdhouse Specifications (in inches)

Information abstracted from Verne Davison's *Attracting Birds*

Species	Entrance diameter	Entrance above floor	Floor dimensions	House depth	Nest above ground (in feet)
Bluebird	1 ½	6–7	5 × 5	8–9	4–10
Chickadee, black-capped	1 ⅛	6–8	4 × 4	8–12	5–50
Creeper, brown	crevices in tree trunks				
Duck, wood[1]					
(metal guard[3])	4	18–19	11–12(dia.)	24	5–15
(wooden guard[3])	3×4 oval	18–19	12 × 12	24	5–15
Flicker[3]	3	14–16	7 × 7	16–24	6–20
Flycatcher, great crested	2	6–8	6 × 6	8–10	8–20
Hawk, sparrow	3	9–12	8 × 8	12–15	10–30
Martin, purple[2]	2 ½	2	7 × 7	7	8–16
Merganser, common	hollow trees				
hooded	hollow trees and nesting boxes				16–30
Owl, barn	6	4	10 × 18	15–18	12–18
saw-whet	2 ½	8–10	6 × 6	10–12	12–20
screech	3	9–12	8 × 8	12–15	10–30
Phoebe	open sides		6 × 6	6	8–12
Robin	open front		6 × 8	8	6–15
Sapsucker	1 ¾	12–16	6 × 6	14–18	12–40
Swallow, barn	open sides		6 × 6	6	8–12
tree[2]	1 ½	1–5	5 × 5	6	10–15
Titmouse, tufted	1 ¼	6–8	4 × 4	8–10	4–15
Woodpecker, downy[3]	1 ¼	6–8	4 × 4	8–10	6–20
hairy[3]	1 ½	9–12	6 × 6	12–16	12–20
red-bellied[3]	2 ½	10–12	6 × 6	12–14	12–50
red-headed[3]	2	9–12	6 × 6	12–15	12–100
Wren, Bewick's	1 ¼	6–8	4 × 4	4–6	6–10
Carolina	1 ¼	4–6	4 × 4	4–8	5–12
house	1–1 ¼	6–8	4 × 4	4–6	5–10
winter	1–1 ¼	6–8	4 × 4	4–6	5–10

[1]Wood duck boxes must be predator-proof (especially from raccoons) to be safe. A 4-inch in diameter metal guard or 4 × 4-inch wooden guard at entrance, or 4-inch horizontal by 3-inch vertical oval guard may be sufficient.
[2]Also uses gourds for nesting.
[3]Add wood shavings or sawdust to 2- or 3-inch depth.

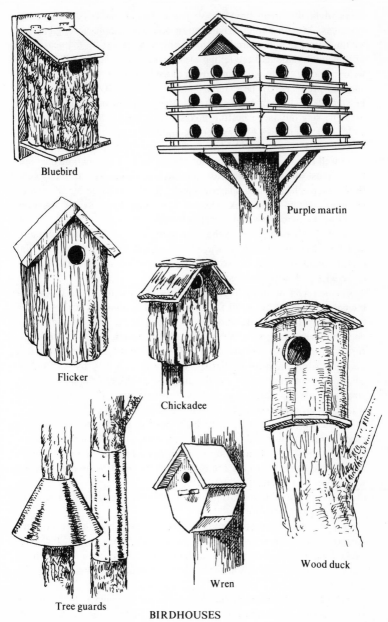

Bluebird

Purple martin

Flicker

Chickadee

Wood duck

Tree guards

Wren

BIRDHOUSES

acres of land a year for the suburbs is having its effect on nesting practices. At a time when urbanization is depriving hole-nesting birds of nesting sites, it is but prudent to fill the gap caused by the scarifying of the countryside and the felling of old trees and fence posts. It is also wise to encourage population growth of useful and disappearing species, such as practiced by Dr. Heinz Meng of New Paltz, New York. To bolster the dwindling sparrow hawk population in his Hudson Valley area, he sets out large nesting boxes with entrance holes three inches wide. Thirteen of his 14 boxes were occupied in 1965.

At least 35 Eastern and Midwestern species use birdhouses, most of them well known and generally much loved birds. They include the bluebird, house wren, chickadees, nuthatches, titmouse, woodpeckers, flicker, screech owl, and sparrow hawk. A few are large birds, such as the barn owl and wood duck. The purple martins, a colony species, often use large, many-chambered, apartment type houses.

Appendix B lists some of the best material available on birdhouses and bird feeders. *Audubon Magazine,* official publication of the National Audubon Society, also provides up-to-date information, both in its articles and in its advertising columns.

Whether you build or buy a birdhouse, it must be of the proper dimensions. (See Table p. 70.) Thousands of birdhouses are produced every year with little attention to the living space and entry aperture needed by various species. A neighbor of ours once received a handsome, rustic birdhouse for Christmas. The family could hardly wait to put it up. Then someone noticed that the floor was only 2 ½ by 3 ½ inches. The minimum floor space for the smallest possible occupant, a house wren or Carolina chickadee, is 4 by 4 inches. A smaller box probably would not give the nestlings sufficient ventilation on hot days.

The nesting box should be strongly built of good wood. A slanting roof for rain run-off and holes in the bottom for drainage are necessary. One side should be detachable to permit easy cleaning. Some biologists now advise against burning the old nest on removal. A helpful parasite which preys on a harmful parasite of the eyes of young birds lays eggs that survive the winter. Burning the nest would destroy the source of future beneficial parasites.

Coconut shells and gourds also make excellent birdhouses and bird feeders. You can grow your own gourds by planting seeds of the long-necked variety in good, well-drained soil. In southern states a familiar sight is a cluster of gourds at the top of a pole, each occupied by a family of martins.

A birdhouse interior should be somewhat roughened to allow the young birds to climb up to the exit. A box for flickers, red-headed wood-

Red tailed hawk

Sparrow hawk

Marsh harrier

Barn owl

Screech owl

peckers, sparrow hawks, or screech owls should have a floor covering of sawdust or shavings.

Put the box where the sunlight can reach it. In the open there is less trouble with cats and other enemies. A perch isn't necessary and may assist enemies of the occupants. Metal guards just below a nest mounted on a post or tree will help to foil cats attempting to raid the birdhouse.

You can help the birds by placing straw, hay, cotton strips, string, and rags in the vicinity of the birdhouse. A supply box may be fastened to a tree, telephone pole, or post, or suspended by wire from a limb to keep cats away.

While metal birdhouses are not normally recommended, one reader of *Audubon Magazine* wrote us that he has had success in using large cans as bluebird houses. The new polyethylene bottles, large size, though unsightly, are also being used.

Many communities, clubs, and societies, as well as individuals, conduct exciting projects to attract certain species of birds. Griggsville, Illinois, has had striking success in attracting purple martins. The Junior Chamber of Commerce put out 28 newly designed aluminum martin houses in 1962, and Griggsville residents set up others. Today Griggsville calls itself the "Purple Martin Capital of the World," with well over 100 martin houses, including one massive structure set up in gratitude for the purple martins' successful control of the mosquito problem. In 1966 Philipsburg, Pennsylvania, and nearby boroughs and townships launched a pilot project with 40 martin houses.

A housewife especially successful in attracting bluebirds is Mrs. Javius K. Matsumoto, of Chappaqua, New York. The Matsumotos have bluebirds every day of the year, sometimes as many as 18 in midwinter. One secret of their success is their supply of millions of mealworms, which they raise in their basement as a staple diet for the bluebirds. These worms are readily raised by alternating layers of bran and paper toweling in a lidded box. Fuller directions are cited in Appendix B.

In the St. Paul, Minnesota, suburbs, John W. Mitchell set out 25 bluebird houses in 35 acres a few years ago. Not until he read *Silent Spring* did he begin to realize why, possibly, he saw few bluebirds any more. He persuaded the Metropolitan Mosquito Control Commission to bypass 160 acres in its insecticide program. Mitchell credits the later presence of a bluebird family to this action.

Bird Nests. It is illegal to remove the nest of a migratory bird even after the nesting season, although the law is rarely enforced. To take a nest one should first get a permit from the U.S. Fish and Wildlife Service. A state permit should also be obtained. It might seem harmless for a boy to

collect nests after the foliage has disappeared and nests become conspicuous against the snow; the wind, rain, and ice eventually will demolish
many of them. Yet, if nest collecting were permitted the privilege might
well be abused. Also, many nests are used by other wildlife after birds
relinquish them, some even by the same birds the following spring.

It is well to know, in addition to the species that nest in birdhouses,
those nesting in trees, hedges, shrubs, grass, and on the ground. If you
are mowing a rarely clipped portion of your property in the spring or
summer, check it for ground-nesting species such as the meadowlark or
bobolink. You may also be endangering nests of game birds such as
the mallard, Hungarian partridge, bobwhite, and ring-necked pheasant.

Bird Feeders. Bird feeding and bird watching are popular winter occupa-
tions. Unlike skiing and skating, you don't have to leave the house to
enjoy them—except to fill the feeders from time to time. There are
excellent feeders on the market—and some poor ones as well. Avoid
anything except a well-built wooden or metal one. The plastic or cardboard feeder is usually not worth the postcard ordering it.

Feeders have the advantage of bringing the birds clearly into view and
making it easy for the birds to eat. Selective feeders keep away unwanted species; sheltered feeders keep the seeds dry. Many people build
their own feeders, while others don't use any, simply placing food on an
outside porch, roof, or windowsill. Squirrels and pigeons do some
poaching, but these interlopers can be dealt with if you really object to
their presence. Personally, I like the squirrels and don't mind the
pigeons unless they become numerous. A hanging feeder may be squirrel
proof unless it is within their jumping distance. Another squirrel-proof
spot for a feeder, if walls are smooth, is an outside windowsill. This may
mean keeping the storm window on the house all summer, but the ring-
side seat for winter visitors is worth it. This feeder should have a glass
top on it to afford a better look at the feathered patrons, and to protect
the food from rain and snow.

Several manufacturers now produce feeders designed to reject any
birds except chickadees and similar small species. Blue jays and house
sparrows are relatively smart, however, and have solved such tactics in
remarkably short order. A glass enclosed feeder that has an admission
hole but 1 $\frac{1}{4}$ inches in diameter will thwart both species.

One ingenious bird attractor uses merely a split log, on one end of
which he straps a jar of peanut butter and on the other a grapefruit.
Mockingbirds like the idea. Some suburban dwellers have been so successful in attracting birds that they have more than they can handle
during snowstorms. To accommodate all visitors, they set up two long

TYPES OF BIRD FEEDERS

planks on wooden horses. When the planks become snow-covered, the birders turn them over and use the other side.

To provide birds with the fat they like during the cold months, drill a small log or branch and place suet in the holes. Then hang the branch vertically. Woodpeckers go for this device. Beef suet is available at most butcher shops at little or no cost.

What else do you feed the birds? Good sunflower seeds, for one thing. Many supermarkets now carry sunflower seeds in one-, two-, or five-pound bags; grain and seed stores may undersell them. Wild bird seed containing millet, corn, sunflower seeds, hemp, and wheat is preferable to plain sunflower seeds (and far cheaper!) if you wish to attract fox sparrows, white-throated sparrows, and slate-colored juncos. Note what sorts of seeds remain uneaten and seek a mixture that does not include these. Many packaged "wild bird seeds" contain seeds little used. Grit is an important ingredient.

Various concoctions of beef suet, bacon fat, and corn meal have also met the birds' approval. Here is one recipe that is designed to attract cardinals, chickadees, titmice, woodpeckers, and nuthatches, but not sparrows and blue jays:

Boil a cup of sugar and a cup of water, add a cup of melted fat, and cool. Mix with corn meal, bread crumbs, bird seed, until very thick. Pack it in a tin can or glass jar and lay the can on its side where the birds can peck at the mixture.

Here is another recipe:

Mix into melted beef-kidney suet peanut butter, yellow corn meal, various bird foods, nuts, and raisins. (Though dubbed "chickadee pie," this appeals to many species.)

Verne E. Davison, a biologist, discovered that only 124 of 742 species that he has studied eat fruits to much extent. He was able to attract only 11 species to feeders with fruit—the bluebird, mockingbird, robin, bobwhite, starling, summer tanager, brown thrasher, wood thrush, cedar waxwing, and red-bellied and red-headed woodpeckers. Only the first three, however, became regular visitors. Dried currants, small raisins, blackberries, black cherries, dogwood fruit, red cedar, and smooth sumac (with peanut butter for mockingbirds) were the much preferred food items.

Nuts are favored by many birds. Find, if you can, a salted nuts supply house. They take back their merchandise when it is no longer fresh and you should be able to buy 100-pound bags at little cost. Manufacturers of peanut butter may also have "peanut hearts," the embryos of the seeds, which are removed and discarded. Though people do not like the flavor, birds seem less particular.

Bobwhites will be encouraged by scattering grain or chick scratch feed on the ground, in an area not too remote from a brush pile or other cover.

If grouse are native to your area they will be attracted to apple trees, whose seeds they will get from fallen fruit and whose buds provide winter food. Wild grapes and bittersweet also provide good grouse food and growth of these vines will be encouraged by killing the tree on which they climb, an end which the vines themselves may bring about. Highbush-cranberry, barberry, the sumacs, black alder, thornapples, birch, and aspen are also good providers of grouse food.

Pheasants will accept whole corn, shelled or on the cob. If cobs are impaled on spikes driven through a 2 × 4 set onto the ground, the food will remain accessible in times of heavy snow.

Winter feeding, to be successful, must be started well before the snow arrives, for many birds establish their feeding areas early. Still more important: if you do feed birds in the autumn don't abandon them when cold weather comes, for they may have become dependent on you.

In bodies of water where summer water levels are relatively stable, ducks may be attracted and held over the breeding season if artificially fed or if suitable duck foods are established. The pondweeds, bur-reeds, arrowheads, watercress and wild rice are favored not only by waterfowl but by fish. Plants from alkaline lakes, however, will not transplant successfully to acid lakes. Recommendations for a diversity of duck food plants suited to different types of shores and waters are well presented in pamphlets provided by the Fish and Wildlife Service, as listed in Appendix B.

The feeding of waterfowl, either at the water's edge or on a lawn near water, will prove interesting though messy. Wood ducks, pintails, and Canada geese may be among your visitors, as well as the ubiquitous mallard. One family, to my knowledge, feeds 150 pounds of grain a day to visiting waterfowl, but some biologists think such practice ill advised in possibly paving the way for disease, and also in building a population too great for local resources of nesting sites.

It is illegal to shoot ducks over an area in which they are fed grain.

Bird Watering Places. Bird baths are often as important in dry summer months as feeders are in winter. The baths should not be so deep that young birds could drown in them. An old garbage can top makes a practical receptacle if a stone is placed in the middle to give suitable footing. More attractive designs are suggested in the accompanying picture and in the references to be found at the end of this book.

Dripping or moving water has an allure for some warblers and other birds. A bucket with a small hole drilled in its bottom and suspended above a catch basin will provide a steady drip. One person in the Chicago area counted 41 species of birds using a drip bird bath in her yard. Twenty other species came into this garden but did not use the bath.

Don't let your bird bath serve as a decoy for cats on the prowl. If the bath basin is in the open, well away from shrubbery or tree limbs, the cats can't easily lie in wait without being detected; yet small birds need an escape shelter from winged predators.

In recent years more and more people are furnishing the birds with heated drinking dishes during the winter. To make such a device, take an eight-inch-square, or larger, wooden box and make a large hole in its top. Fit a plastic bowl for water into the hole and place a 25-watt light bulb on an extension cord into the box and under the plastic dish to keep the water from freezing.

Bird Roosts. The prevalence and wide use of birdhouses undoubtedly indicates a shortage of natural nesting cavities for bird life. The use of bird roost boxes reflects an extension of the same trend, caused by increasing urbanization. Since it is difficult for birds to find good roosting shelter, suburban residents can help them by building roosting boxes. These are much like birdhouses, except that the entry hole is at the bottom and the interior has staggered perches extending from the sides. As many as 31 Carolina wrens have been found jammed into one birdhouse trying to keep warm. A well placed roost could be even warmer and roomier.

Planting for Birds. Certain trees and shrubs greatly help to attract birds for nest sites, food, and hiding places. Some also provide flowers, fruits, and autumn color.

Among the evergreens, pines are favored by some 63 species of birds that feed on the cones and roost or nest in these trees. White pine and Swiss stone pine are especially recommended. Good for nesting and for seeds are hemlocks and hollies.

The shrubby dogwoods (red osier and gray dogwood) have attracted as many as 93 species of birds. The flowering dogwood, considered by many the most attractive small tree in the country, magnolias, flowering crabapples, and mulberry trees are also high on the bird food list.

A fast-growing hedge plant, the multiflora rose, has been widely introduced and acclaimed in this country. Not only does it grow swiftly and produce attractive flowers and berries, but it also forms a natural habitat for a wide diversity of wildlife. A 300-yard multiflora rose hedge planted from seedlings in 1953 near Dayton, Ohio, had become a high, dense tangle by 1958, excellent as a fence barrier. Its red berries attracted 11 species of birds. The cardinal, catbird, mockingbird, and field sparrow, as well as the short-tailed shrew, meadow mouse, and woodchuck made homes in it. A winter study revealed 12 abandoned wasp nests, 15 egg cases of praying mantises, and 60 moth cocoons.

Despite its many good qualities, the multiflora rose has become controversial because of its jungle-like character, its persistence, and tendency to spread. Robert F. Scott of the Bureau of Sport Fisheries and Wildlife, has reported that "multiflora has developed into an appreciable nuisance over much of its introduced range." He said the plant has caused problems in eight of nine Midwest States and is being bulldozed out in several states. Agreement on the so-called nuisance character of multiflora rose is far from complete, however. Of 43 Maryland farmers interviewed in 11 counties, Mr. Scott said, only 30 percent

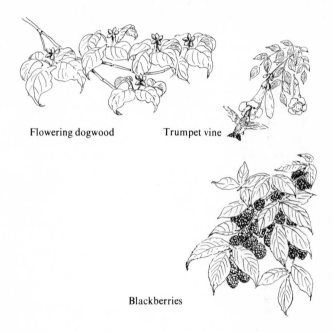

Flowering dogwood   Trumpet vine

Blackberries

had definite complaints. Another 15 percent were equivocal. "At least one" of the 43 farmers was bitter about having planted it and wanted it eradicated. The conclusion seems to be that multiflora is a fine plant for wildlife but should be planted sparingly and carefully controlled unless you have abundant land on which it can spread.

Dozens of excellent plants will lend attractiveness to your property as well as serve wildlife. Some of the best for ornamental and birding purposes are:

American holly *(Ilex opaca)*   flowering crabapple *(Pyrus* sp.*)*
inkberry *(Ilex glabra)*   azalea *(Azalea* sp.*)*
black-alder *(Alnus glutinosa)*   mountain laurel *(Kalmia latifolia)*
magnolia *(Magnolia* sp.*)*   rhododendron *(Rhododendron* sp.*)*

Living With Your Land

highbush-cranberry (*Viburnum trilobum*)	shadbush (*Amelanchier canadensis*)
scarlet firethorn (*Pyracantha coccinea*)	arrow-wood (*Viburnum dentatum*)
Russian olive (*Elaeagnus angustifolia*)	red-berried elder (*Sambucus pubens*)
viburnums (*Viburnum sieboldii, V. dilatatum, V. opulus*)	blueberry (*Vaccinium* sp.)
	American mountain ash (*Sorbus americana*)

Your chances of attracting a covey of quail, if they occur nearby, are excellent if you set out shrub lespedeza plants intended for your geographical area. Fortunately they don't appeal to rodents and non-game birds. Lespedezas are nitrogen-rich legumes, invaluable for building up depleted soils and in gullies. The lespedeza that grows farthest north is natob. This is a strain of bicolor lespedeza that is suitable for most parts of the states of the Middle Atlantic Seaboard. Japonica lespedeza ranges from New Jersey to western Missouri. Complete directions for growing lespedezas are available in a Department of Agriculture leaflet cited below (Davison 1965).

If you plant mulberries or black cherry trees, place them far from the house as the fruit stains clothes and floors easily. Most of the popular birds—some 68 species—relish mulberries. Other choices of the fruit-eating birds are blackberry, wild grape, elderberry, cherry elaeagnus, dogwood, autumn olive, bulueberry, and pokeberry. You also might choose to grow your own sunflower seeds, browntop, millet, wheat, and corn for bird use.

Nut-eating birds favor oak, beech, hickory, pine, and walnut trees. The birds don't crack the nuts, but will feed after squirrels and other animals have opened them. For insect-eating birds, well-kept, well-fertilized lawns are helpful, along with brushy fence rows and a diversity of trees.

The food preferences of each of some 40 species of birds that may frequent the yard in the eastern half of this country were published in successive issues of *Audubon Magazine* starting with the September-October issue of 1965. Included were the types of plant life, if any, preferred by each bird species.

Bird Care. An invariable question in the suburbs is, "What do you do with orphaned, injured, or sick birds?" The "orphaned" birds may not actually be orphaned; the parent birds probably are around or will return. They usually can take better care of the fledgling than you can. If possible, place the bird back in the nest, or as close to the nest as you can. It isn't true that parent birds will abandon young that have been touched by humans.

It is illegal to hold a migratory bird captive, but I know of no instance where action has been taken when the bird was sick, injured, or helpless. In some communities a bird hospital is provided with a permit from the Fish and Wildlife Service—sometimes at the request of a National Audubon Society branch.

An unfeathered young bird should have artificial heat day and night, and be fed every 20 minutes during daylight hours. No liquid should be given it. Blue jays, cardinals, flickers, grackles, mockingbirds, red-winged blackbirds, shrikes, sparrows, and woodpeckers thrive on a rotating diet of fresh fruit, especially grapes (oranges to woodpeckers, warblers, cardinals, and orioles only), an egg mixture, hamburger, mealworms, and a "salad" of grated carrots, chopped celery leaves, and watercress. Young robins will accept earthworms and ground beef. Nighthawks should get hamburger and mealworms; doves and pigeons egg mixture and pigeon seed. Raw beef and chicken are suitable for hawks and owls.

When the bird has regained its health, let it forage for itself in the yard. Finally release it—in the habitat to which its species is accustomed.

Window Collisions. Birds often are casualties from flying into the glass of windows which mirror the sky. Netting stretched over glass, or leather thongs hung before it will eliminate accidents. A few ribbons or strips of crepe paper hung inside a large window, or an ornamental "sun catcher," should also prevent fly-in. In Germany, hawk or owl silhouettes pasted on windows are reported to cause birds to wheel off a collision course. Small suet feeders held to the glass by suction cups should not only successfully signal the presence of a barrier but bring chickadees almost into the room.

Bird Nuisances. Compared to their value in controlling garden pests, the damage caused by birds is relatively slight. The Department of Agriculture has placed the value of American bird life at $350,000,000 annually. This purely economic factor disregards the equally valid aesthetic and scientific values. When we read of crop raids by some species, we are getting only one side of the story. Crows and grackles may wreak havoc in a cornfield and robins may denude cherry trees, but these same species make up for their transgressions in multiple ways. The omnivorous crows help to reduce carrion, empty mouse nests, and lower the population of beetle larvae. Red-winged blackbirds, grackles, and starlings, though nuisances at times, consume enormous quantities of harmful insects. Many species catch large numbers of insects in feeding their young.

Occasionally members of the woodpecker family attempt to take over human habitations. In one case flickers and hairy woodpeckers kept a Midwest resident patching up his siding where the birds had drilled holes under the eaves of his gables, ignoring the six woodpecker houses he had supplied them in the yard. He was advised to paint his house with creosote or install spinners on it such as those used in celebrating the opening of a new gasoline station.

In late summer or early fall enormous flocks of starlings may congregate in roost trees, and if these are near a residence may be encouraged to move on. Shooting is a fairly successful method, but the flocks often contain large numbers of purple martins, robins, and red-winged blackbirds, birds that should not, and may not legally, be killed. Gassing is impractical. Trimming the trees will encourage the birds to find another site. Some communities have had at least temporary success by broadcasting the alarm calls of starlings; recordings and equipment are available from Jennings Industries (Appendix A), which also has recordings for use against bird flocks of other species in agricultural areas and airports.

Considered a non-migratory bird, the starling, as well as its nest and young, is not protected by the Migratory Bird Treaty. Several responsible authorities, therefore, suggest that the bird's population be controlled by destruction of the starling's nest and young. The National Audubon Society takes a dim view of shooting, poisoning, or otherwise destroying any bird life. One extreme measure often leads to another when man tries to take nature into his own hands.

A leaflet, *Trapping Starlings* (1965), says the most effective trap is a modification of the Australian crow trap. This is in the shape of an open bottomed V. The birds respond to bait by dropping through the point of the V. Once in, they go to the sides and can't find the opening. These traps generally are five or six feet high, six feet wide, and eight feet long. Live birds are used as decoys. The Fish and Wildlife Service advises the use of a fumigant to kill the captives. It also advises on the use of automatic exploders, electric shock, metal projectors, whirling devices, fireworks, protective netting, revolving lights, and sound—techniques more applicable to city roosts. Manufacturers who sell these items and small bird traps are listed in the Fish and Wildlife Service Leaflet 409.

The Service has published leaflets on the control of other so-called nuisance birds. To prevent the nesting of unwanted species, the Service advises homeowners to remove nests of these species every two weeks. Strands of wire stretched on flat or slightly slanting roofs, 45° shields to block off cornices, and large sheets of plastic or netting hung over possible roosts are effective moves a homeowner may wish to make. A doorbell in the roosting area hooked up so the bell may be sounded at will, or sharp-pointed wires or prongs are also pigeon, starling and sparrow discouragers.

A product named Avitrol, available through licensed exterminator companies, is alleged to be effective against pigeons, sparrows, starlings, and cowbirds. It involves feeding the birds chemically treated foods which, through producing behavior disturbances, disrupts flocking behavior.

Toad

Leopard frog

Green frog tadpole

7. *Snakes, Turtles, Toads, and Fish*

Amphibians and reptiles, being cold-blooded, will not be evident in the winter months; but when there is yet a fringe of ice on the ponds a careful observer may discover small milky stalks of jelly-like substance on the leafy bottom. This is a sign that the male salamanders have left their winter quarters, for the milky stalks are the sperm cases that the males have deposited. The females soon follow the males and engulf these sperm cases with their vents to become fertilized. The egg masses of these larger salamanders float or are attached to twigs or debris in the pond. For most persons, however, the first evidence of the reactivation of the cold-bloods, and an assurance that spring is on its way, is the chorus of spring peepers and cricket frogs. It is a chorus soon added to by the larger frogs and the melodious-voiced toads. In this season too the turtles will appear in the ponds, and snakes may be discovered in sunny places.

Turtles. There are many turtles in our area that one may wish to know and for that purpose one should obtain one or more of the books listed in Appendix B. Here we need consider but three species whose habits or character deserve special mention: the snapper, the soft shell, and the box turtle.

Handling any water-dwelling turtle is not without some risk, and it is wise to wash one's hands thoroughly after picking one up. The commercially sold green sliders, painted turtles, and baby snappers are particularly suspect. In 1964 the Minnesota Health Department, investigating an outbreak of abdominal infections, traced 22 cases of gastroenteritis to infected pet turtles. Most of the patients were children. Six patients required hospitalization, one suffered septicemia. Salmonella has been identified as the infecting agent in Michigan.

Turtles for the market are caught in southern waters which are likely to be contaminated, or their eggs are hatched in gardens fertilized by animal excreta. On the turtle farms the animals are often fed unclean material. To avoid infection keep turtle water out of the kitchen area and do not use a turtle container for other purposes. Wash thoroughly after servicing the turtle bowl, and keep other pets from drinking the turtle's water.

Painting turtle backs is cruel for it inhibits growth in the painted area and results in deformity. The marketing of decorated young turtles is a vulgarity that should be stopped by complaints to the store manager, a local humane society and boycott. Needless to say, carving a live turtle's shell should not be tolerated nor the drilling of a hole through the shell margin for purposes of tethering. Turtles, though silent, are not without feeling.

Trapping turtles for the sake of reducing their numbers in a pond or for cooking has many advocates. In some areas there are professional turtle trappers whose service you might enlist, but if you want to do it yourself you can make a turtle trap of heavy chicken wire with a funnel-shaped opening and a dead fish placed inside. Such a trap is of course placed underwater. Another type is made by sinking a barrel, perforated to admit water, with its open end toward the sky. A crawl board hinged

Box turtle

Snapping turtle

Softshell turtle

on the barrel's rim may be so balanced as to tip into the barrel a turtle that has attained the plank's end. A light spring hinge within the circumference of the barrel should improve its effectiveness. This sort of trap is, however, unsuited to snappers, which are not prone to sun themselves.

Snapping turtles inhabit ponds, lakes, and streams where they feed upon fish, ducks, and carrion. They are most usually noticed as they lie submerged in the water with only the upper part of the head showing, or on land when they are out searching for a dry, well-drained site on which to deposit their eggs. They are easily recognized by their large heads, rough and often alga-covered backs, long saw-tooth tails, and bad tempers. Snappers may grow to a shell length of over 12 inches and attain a weight of 35 pounds. They may be picked up by their tails but should be held well away from the body, with their undersurface toward one's leg. Their long necks, strong jaws, and quick action make them too dangerous for a child to handle. The meat of a snapper is excellent, and some fanciers will keep them in a barrel, fattening them until time for harvest.

The soft-shelled turtles are encountered in some lakes but are essentially river dwellers. Though almost exclusively aquatic, they are swift runners on land. They are recognized by their flat leathery shells, and sharp pointed heads on long necks. Sharp jaws and claws combined with quick tempers make them dangerous to handle, particularly when they approach their maximum size of 18 inches and 35 pounds. The soft-shelleds are esteemed by gourmets.

The box turtle is probably the most interesting member of this group for it is terrestrial and docile, as well as exhibiting the remarkable ability of shutting itself completely within its shell by closing up its hinged hatches, fore and aft. It is long-lived, perhaps to 100 years. A satisfactory garden pet, it will feed upon insects, worms, hamburger, and a wide variety of plant material. Of course it will need to be fenced in for you may enjoy its company more than it does yours.

Snakes. There are 224 forms of snakes in the United States and Canada. All of them are harmless except the rattlesnakes, copperhead, cottonmouth, and coral snake. The only venomous snakes well within the region of our concern are the timber and massasauga rattlesnakes and the copperhead. Other forms of rattlesnakes and the cottonmouth are to be found on the western or southern fringes of this territory. Proper manuals will identify the species and their ranges.

The risk of snakebite is minuscule, but the results of a bite are too serious to ignore. Though the suburbs are encroaching on the timber

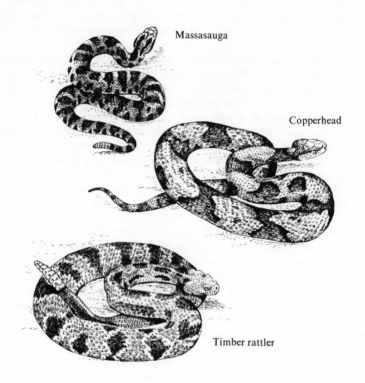

Massasauga

Copperhead

Timber rattler

Water moccasin

rattler and copperhead habitats the odds are heavily against the average rural dweller ever seeing either species. The timber rattler, which often grows to a length of four and one-half feet, is yellowish, and typically has dark V-shaped bands on its back and a darker tail terminating in a horny rattle. Dark to black phases also occur. It is aggressive if molested and must be carefully avoided. All snakes that rattle their tails are not rattlers, however, for some others vibrate their tail tips among dry leaves, producing thus a noise similar to a rattlesnake's.

The massasauga is a smaller rattlesnake, attaining a length of about three feet. It is not uncommon in the Great Lakes region and toward the southwest. Though its favored home is in the low wetlands it is encountered occasionally on higher drier ground. The massasauga is a brownish-gray snake with dark blotches along the back and smaller spots along the sides.

The copperhead of the north is distinguished by its coppery color, hour-glass-shaped darker blotches set transversely, and spotted sides of the belly. The young have yellow tails. A rapid vibration of the tail when the snake is alarmed is characteristic. With all poisonous snakes one should keep one's distance, even from a head that has been cut off. The reflex to bite persists for some time.

The more common snakes are likely to be beneficial and feed on rodents or insects. It is well to learn to recognize the garter snakes often encountered about homes, the dark water snakes which though harmless are looked upon by many as "moccasins," and the hog-nosed snake or "puff adder" which when treatened will spread out its neck, cobra-fashion, hiss and strike, yet will not bite. If its bluffing fails it may roll over and play dead. This snake and a few others do well in captivity, but a knowledge of their normal diet is essential if they are to be kept confined. Green snakes are prodigious insect eaters. Rat snakes and milk snakes, so called because they are often found in pastures (needless to state, they do not milk cows), are known as house snakes in some areas—affectionately so by people familiar with them. The miniature ring-necked, brown, and red-bellied snakes become unafraid as captives though each of them, like the garter snakes, will emit unpleasant odors when first handled. In nature they keep down infestations of slugs and some insects.

Snakebite. The timber and massasauga rattlesnakes, the northern copperhead, and the western cottonmouth are among the least venomous snakes. Their venom is less dangerous than that of most poisonous snakes in other parts of the country and they have far less of it. In a 1962 list of snakes that "have been implicated in fatal bites to humans," Dr.

Findlay E. Russell, co-author of a snakebite manual for the Armed Forces, lists none of the four species. However, there is always the *possibility* of death, especially to children. Death is not the only consideration; improper treatment may require surgery, and even long hospitalization is an unwelcome possibility.

Snakebite First Aid. Symptoms: Fang marks are one sign of a venomous snakebite but it is sometimes difficult to distinguish them from tooth marks of a large non-venomous snake. A timber rattlesnake bite usually causes swelling in five minutes, but swelling may not be evident after a copperhead or massasauga bite. A timber rattler's bite is likely to be painful, but copperhead and massasauga bites may cause no pain for several hours, according to Dr. Russell. Discolored skin usually accompanies the swelling as venom often destroys some tissue in the bite region.

First aid and subsequent treatment recommended by Dr. Russell may be summarized as follows: Remove rings and bracelets from the bitten extremity. Take the victim to a hospital for snakebite serum injections. Keep him quiet and reassured. Give him beverages but no alcohol. The snake should be killed, if possible, and taken to the hospital to assure proper choice of antivenin. A light tourniquet is advisable on an arm, leg, hand, or foot but should be fully released for 90 seconds every 10 minutes. No tourniquet should ever be loosened suddenly, for the sudden flow of venom might kill the patient.

Quarter-inch to half-inch incisions across the fang marks will help to promote removal of venom by suction. Incisions about a quarter of an inch deep should be made with a disinfected knife or razor blade. Make no more than four cuts. Extraction of the venom by use of a suction cup or by mouth should be started at once and continued for 30 to 60 minutes. Suction started more than 30 minutes after the bite is futile.

Medical authorities warn that prolonged refrigeration of the bitten area is dangerous and ineffective. Ice packs are approved for only short periods while the patient is awaiting medical attention or to alleviate pain but never as a substitute for the first aid and later treatment recommended.

Scout leaders and others exposed to poison snake habitats should know how to administer antivenin, but it is better done by a doctor. Beyond first aid measures it is unwise to attempt curative action.

Control of Snakes. A well-kept lawn, neat shrubbery, absence of litter and debris, and the filling of holes and crevices will discourage snakes from becoming tenants on your property. Without shelter, snakes move elsewhere. Creosote may be used as a repellent without harm to wildlife or humans. Snake-tight fences for children's playing areas deserve consideration in areas of high snake population.

If there is reason to believe that there are poisonous snakes in the vicinity, wear boots or leggings when you go into rougher lands. If you don't have leggings, wear the trouser legs outside the boots. Because poisonous snakes are active at night it is unwise to go into their territory in the dark unequipped with a good light. Your state conservation or fish and game department should provide helpful advice on the need and techniques of snake control.

Frogs. A land holder with frogs nearby is fortunate, for they are harvesters of insects and provide one of the most welcome sounds of spring. There is no reason to discourage their presence and not a great deal to be done to encourage them other than to maintain a pond or rough edge on a lake or stream shore. All species succumb easily to DDT sprays that may have been applied in the area, and tree frogs, some of the most attractive, seem particularly vulnerable. These, after their egg laying season in the water, move out through the shrubbery, and their clear bell-like voices will grace a garden and perhaps mystify the searcher as to the singers' whereabouts.

Adult frogs may be kept easily in any aquarium if you provide a dry resting place and clear water, with an ample food supply, usually of live insects or worms. The tree frogs have suction pads on their toes and can climb the glass sides of an aquarium so it must be screened. Tadpoles may be kept in any aquarium but there must be some algae present, and, since tadpoles become frogs (or toads), there must be a place for them to emerge.

To know the frogs, start with a simple manual. Recordings of amphibian voices will help you identify them by sound.

Toads. Toads are one of nature's most efficient insect destroyers. One toad may fill its stomach four times a day. Encourage them around your garden; greenhouse keepers sometimes keep toads as unpaid assistants. Though land dwellers for most of the year, they must, like most other amphibians, return to water for mating and egg laying, and in a pond may assemble in tremendous numbers; then their paired strings of eggs may be seen in the shallows. Toads don't cause warts but a milky secretion of their skin is poisonous and will irritate the mucous tissue of mouth and eyes, so wash your hands after handling one.

Salamanders. These animals, occasionally thought of as lizards, are readily distinguished from those reptiles in having smooth moist skins.

93

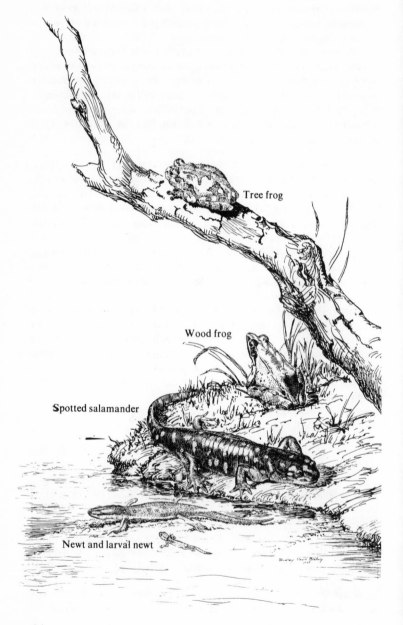

Tree frog

Wood frog

Spotted salamander

Newt and larval newt

Most of the score or so of types that occur in this area are quite small and will never be encountered without a search through rotting logs or other moisture-retaining habitats. The mudpuppy, which grows to 12 inches, is occasionally taken by fishermen. The hellbender grows to 20 inches. Both are completely aquatic and neither, popular belief to the contrary, is poisonous. The spotted and tiger salamanders, whose length will exceed eight inches, are found on land, sometimes in the leafy debris of cellar holes into which they have fallen. The newts are the only other species likely to be seen about. During one to three years of their youth, when they are known as efts, they wander about on land seeking insects and other small prey, even by day in moist weather. An eft is orange-red to dark red, with brighter red spots on its back, and is about three inches long. When adult it returns to the water, develops a flat swimming tail, becomes olive green with red spots, and never again returns to land. In both life stages newts make satisfactory aquarium or terrarium pets and will accept small meat scraps as well as live food.

Of Fish. Few landowners are fortunate enough to have properties in which fishing improvement action is possible, and such persons will want to refer to special books on the subject, such as Lagler's (as cited), or to seek the professional advice to their state game department. If you have a stream you can dam it or create deep holes by dredging or alteration of the stream course. Creation of riffles will aerate the water and improve it and will also create breeding places for additional types of fish foods. Stream development may go hand in hand with erosion control plans. Such alterations should fit in with planting plans.

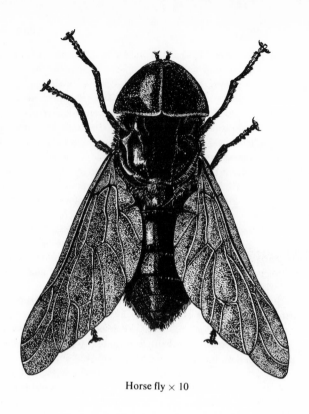

Horse fly × 10

8. The Lower Animals

Animals without backbones present forms of wondrous and endless diversity. They are essential parts of the reticulum of life that over many millions of years has evolved in harmony with the land. Each species is as a thread in this web, and the strength of the whole is closely related to presence of an intact fabric. If one interferes too drastically with the biota, new problems arise. Spray against the cankerworm or bark beetles and you will kill the insect-harvesting birds too. Then you may expect an outbreak of scale insects, which in turn will need another sort of spray to save the trees.

Insects are the only pollinating agents for many plants, red clover and native orchids among them. Without the appropriate carrier of pollen the plants would produce no seed and so become extinct. Other insects are of importance in reducing dung and carrion to soil ingredients. Some perform an essential role in destroying dead trees, others are important as fish food. Many may give us pleasure through the mere fact of their great beauty. Perhaps you or your young would be interested in joining the ranks of the amateur entomologists, many of whom have made important contributions to science while indulging in a healthy avocational pursuit. References which follow can guide you to such a course.

Although city dwellers are familiar with mosquitoes, flies, and gnats, a move to the country is likely to involve greater exposure to such nuisances inasmuch as more leisure time will be spent out-of-doors, and country or suburban premises usually, in season, produce more pest insects in greater variety.

The world of the invertebrates is much too great to be dealt with briefly though some of the more common brushes with this section of the animal world in suburban and country life are dealt with here. Only a small percentage of people in the suburbs and country will suffer any severe damage or even inconvenience from insects. I would not wish to discourage a prospective purchaser of property beyond the city limits, yet an occasional word of caution is called for, particularly in relation to the avoidance or treatment of stings and the possibility of infection from an animal-borne disease. Fortunately malaria, once a scourge in the north, has been wiped out over the territory we consider, and this part of the country is not plagued with many of the animal troubles of warmer climates. First attention may be given to the stinging insects.

Some people are so sensitive to the venom from stinging insects that death could occur quickly without proper treatment, and sometimes does even with the best treatment. In the northern United States, stinging insects are a greater danger to life than are venomous snakes. From 1952 to 1954, 86 people in this country died from insect stings, 71 from snake bites, and 39 from spider bites. Bees, hornets, yellow jackets, and wasps, the greatest offenders, are also of great biological value either as pollinating agents or as insect pest destroyers. They are not to be condemned, just avoided.

Hornets are half-inch black insects that build football-sized paper nests in trees or shrubs, or attach them to buildings. If the nests are in a place where you may occasionally disturb the occupants you might use an aerosol hornet spray (which is designed to send the insecticide eight feet or more), applying it at night or in cold weather when the insects are inactive. In some places the nest may be burned, using a kerosene soaked torch at the end of a long pole, but do not attempt this without wearing a headnet, stout gloves, and adequate body covering. A nest attached to a house may be so placed as to be quickly raked into a container which may then be covered and the insects destroyed.

Wasps are narrow-waisted black, brown or red insects an inch or less in length. There are several species here, some building nests of mud, others of paper. The common wasp has uncased paper brood combs which contain no food, the young being fed by the adults. These nests may be sprayed and then raked off.

Yellow Jackets. Their waspish forms and yellow-banded abdomens will identify them. The nests, of paper, are sometimes like the hornets', at other times built in woodpiles or in the ground. Kerosene or lye will doom the digger yellow jackets when poured into the ground nests. Nests in the open may be treated as are hornet nests.

Honey bees, unlike the species named above, cannot sting repeatedly, though this is of small comfort to the person stung. The honey bee dies after leaving its barbed stinger, including venom sac, in the victim. Avoid breaking the venom sac, and remove it immediately after being stung. A swift scrape of the fingernail will remove the stinger and sac before the venom can be injected. This is better than plucking out the stinger with fingers or tweezers, an action likely to squeeze in more venom.

Sting treatment and preventive measures. Death can occur swiftly in persons sensitive to insect stings, and immediate medical attention may be essential. Difficulty in breathing, extreme weakness, shock and semi-consciousness are among the symptoms. In serious cases, use a tourniquet or ice packs to slow the spread of the venom. Get the victim an adrenalin shot at any cost. Persons subject to severe reactions should carry self-injection adrenalin ampules, or an adrenalin inhaler. A few whiffs may stave off the sting effects sufficiently to let the victim reach a hospital for further treatment. Immunization shots with insect venom extract have proven highly successful in a study made of 2,606 insect-sensitive persons in 1964. In less severe cases, a baking soda paste or cold packs of household ammonia will help to ease the pain.

Individuals sensitive to insect stings should do little gardening without taking immunization shots. Do not use perfumes, hair tonic, and other

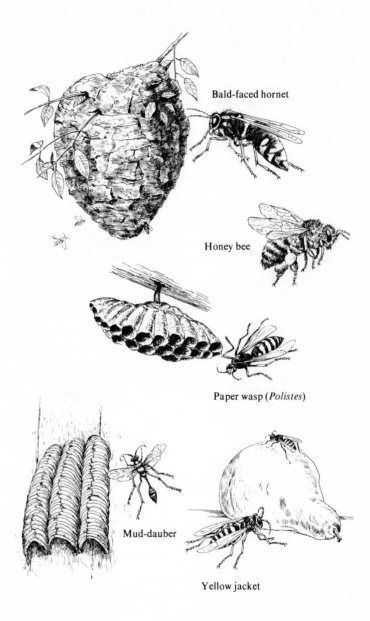

Bald-faced hornet

Honey bee

Paper wasp (*Polistes*)

Mud-dauber

Yellow jacket

cosmetics attractive to insects; and avoid quick, sudden actions if stinging insects appear. White apparently is less attractive to these insects, so
don't wear dark, floppy clothes, and always wear shoes. Keep the garbage can areas clean and food covered, or yellow jackets may gather.

Flies. Flies come in many sizes and varieties. Some, through unclean
feeding habits or unclean breeding places, may transmit diseases. Others
—the deer flies, horse flies, and dog flies among them—are biters and
can make summer days unpleasant. Black flies, which breed in running
water, have a relatively short season, but a tormenting one. There are,
however, some very beneficial predatory flies, like those whose larvae
feed on scale insects and others that feed on gypsy moth larvae.

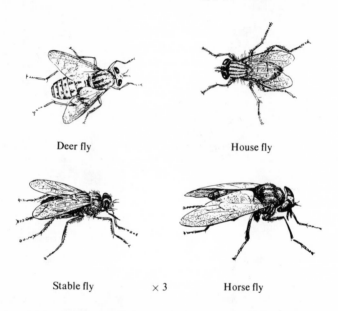

Deer fly   House fly

Stable fly   × 3   Horse fly

Some other groups of insects, "flies" in name only, have marked
importance. Among these are the dragonflies, which, both as larvae (in
the water) and adults, feed on small insects. Sawflies are serious
defoliators of trees, and sometimes reach epidemic populations with disastrous results to forests.

Repellents and screening are the best defenses against all flies, but fly
traps, suitably baited, will produce impressive results. Because such traps
attract flies from afar their usefulness may be more psychological than

exterminative for not all flies will enter the traps and you might be just building up a larger local population.

Mosquitoes. Mosquito control may be beyond your reach for mosquitoes are strong fliers and a good wind may carry them miles from their breeding place. Yet to control mosquitoes on your premises you should find their local breeding places, which are always standing water. Clean bird baths at least once a week. See that rain barrels, cisterns, and septic tanks are tightly sealed. Keep rain gutters clean. Fill in stagnant pools and tree holes with concrete.

If standing water must be kept, you may kill the mosquito larvae by applying a bit of kerosene or fuel oil, 2 to 4 ounces for each 100 square feet or 7 to 14 gallons per acre. Do not, however, use this material where there is emergent vegetation; it may kill the plants and prove ineffective against the mosquitoes. Several insecticides are also effective but the danger in their use does not commend them. A light mist spray of a pyrethrum oil solution, sometimes available in garden supply stores, may be safely used in fish ponds. Formulas which also contain DDT or other "modern" insecticides will kill the fish. For further recommendations consult the government bulletin cited in Appendix B.

Beetles. Your property may well be the home of over 1,000 species of beetles; world wide they number in excess of a quarter million. Your quota may include such beneficial species as carrion beetles and the ladybird beetles, which feed on the destructive aphids (plant lice), but may also number some destructive species such as the Japanese beetle, rose chafers, and weevils. If you have a beetle problem you may seek the aid of your county agent who should help identify the culprit and recommend corrective measures.

Carpet Beetles. Although this is not a book directed towards household problems and carpet beetles are no strangers to city life, a word about them will not be amiss since they are possibly the most destructive of all insects. The adults feed only out-of-doors on flower pollen but their larvae will eat most anything of organic origin: furs, carpets, silks, cottons, furniture filling, and so on. There are several species but the hairy larvae all bear a family resemblance. Once you recognize their presence, by larvae or their shed skins, do not delay corrective measures; they are not easy to eradicate. DDT sprays and chlordane have proved effective in repeated applications a few days apart but most practical is the removal and destruction of the infested object or complete fumiga-

Carpet beetle and its destructive larva.

Ladybird beetle   Japanese beetle

tion in a tightly sealed container. For household use Paracide (para-dichlorabenzine) is effective and relatively safe.

Ants. Ants out-of-doors will not concern you except as a source of house infestation. Large carpenter ants may be brought in with firewood and it is well not to carry in, except directly to the fire, any wood visibly

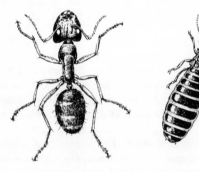

Carpenter ant   King termite

The ants, like their cousins the wasps, have slender waists. Termites have sturdier lines.

infected. These black ants may also move into the house on their own and may tunnel small areas of porches or arbors. They should not be confused with termites from which they may be readily distinguished by having narrow "waists." The tunnels of carpenter ants are clean, almost polished, and cut across the grain of the wood. Termite tunnels contain no sawdust, and tend to follow the grain of the wood. To rid premises of carpenter ants find where they come from by observing their travels. The colony, if in firewood, may be destroyed by spraying with a weak solution of DDT or chlordane powder. Nests in a building structure may be treated by injecting an oil solution of either dieldrin or chlordane.

Smaller ants can be difficult to eliminate but by systematically poisoning all ant nests near the house foundations and persistently poisoning with two or three types of commercial ant poisons within the areas that you see them it is possible to avoid calling in the exterminator. Be sure to read the instructions on the poison containers carefully and follow them. *Ants in Home and Garden* (see Appendix B) gives further advice.

Termites, or "white ants," are a problem in some areas of the North. In buying or building a house insist that the foundation be equipped with a termite shield. In areas where termites are known to be prevalent the Federal Housing Administration requires either a chemical or physical barrier as a method of termite protection in all new construction it insures. Its standards are available on request to the FHA. If you have termites within a building it is best to call on the services of a licensed exterminator.

Fleas. Of the many species of fleas but three are likely to seek you out: the dog flea, human flea, and rat flea. Repellents (which see) are effective but eliminating the offenders is better. To rid a dog or cat of fleas, commercial flea powders are available, or one may dust-in powdered derris root mixed with two parts corn starch or flour, repeating the treatment in ten days. Pyrethrum powder may be used the same way. The animal should be treated over papers onto which the stupefied fleas will drop. The paper with its fleas may then be burned. As preventive measures do not let your pets sleep under a house where fleas may abound, or else keep the pets always out-of-doors.

Fleas may become established in a house, where they breed in floor cracks, under carpets, or in inadequately swept areas. Places on which a dog or cat habitually sleeps are particularly subject to infection. Naphthalene flakes spread about the room followed by closing off the room for 24 hours will help rid the premises of these pests. Fleas may be trapped by putting a small light over a pan of water covered with a thin film of kerosene.

Insects affecting shade and ornamental trees, shrubs, and garden plants are far too varied for treatment in a book of this size, and it is recommended that particular problems be referred to your state or local forester or county agricultural agent. The Department of Agriculture and many state agencies publish pamphlets dealing with these problems, and inquiries directed there usually receive prompt attention.

Gypsy moths. The gypsy moths' vast numbers are worse than their bite. A heavy infestation on deciduous trees may strip off the leaves, but one may be far more concerned about the millions of caterpillars crawling up the house, or dropping from trees. The trees rarely die. Gypsy moth outbreaks, though untidy, are no threat to public health, and cause no immediately severe financial loss.

Tent Caterpillars. These familiar invaders which set up their own shelters in trees and shrubs reach boom populations every seventh year or so. The tents are easy to see, to knock down, or to burn out with a kerosene soaked torch. Several species of birds (cuckoos, orioles) feed heavily on this colonial insect. The tent caterpillar quickly develops resistance to insecticides.

Cankerworms. Like the gypsy moth, cankerworms cause much discomfiture. Swinging on their silken threads, they make mass descents on the suburbs. DDT spraying in some areas killed off the natural predators of the cankerworm, which then developed a population explosion. The worms destroy tree foliage but can be stopped by proper action taken in early spring (even in February) and fall. The adults emerge from the ground in early spring. The wingless females crawl up tree trunks and there are discovered by small gray winged males after which the eggs are laid in the bark crevices. The leaves of the tree appear and the larvae hatch at about the same time, and the results of the worms' feeding are soon apparent.

One can keep the adult females from reaching their egg-laying site by painting a roadblock around the trunk, using a sticky substance called *Tree Tanglefoot,* available at garden supply houses. If you don't want to mark the tree, make a two-inch band of cotton batting and wrap it around the trunk, holding it in place with tar paper and tacks, then spread the *Tanglefoot* thickly on the band. If you don't have the cotton batting, use a paper strip with shredded wood liner sometimes sold under the trade name of *Tree Balsam.* The band should be in place by mid-

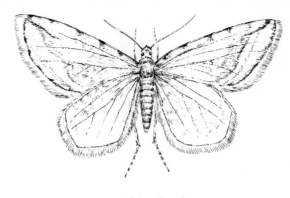

Adult male × 3

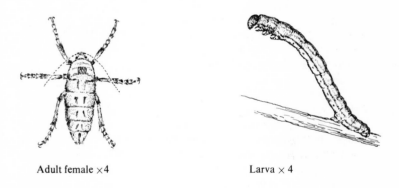

Adult female ×4   Larva × 4

Spring cankerworm

October and kept there until the ground freezes. Renew it when the ground thaws and keep the band sticky until after apple blossom time. This generally thwarts infestations by both the spring and fall cankerworms. A band of contact insecticide applied on the trunk is said also to be effective.

Periodical Cicadas. One of the most interesting but infrequent insect visitations is that of the periodical cicada, often called the 17-year locust. Nationally, there are several broods of cicada, some recurring every 13

Periodical cicada

years, but the most numerous is that with a 17-year cycle. In the cicada's year of emergence holes around trees begin sprouting large, crawling larvae. Fat after years of nourishment in the ground, they crawl up the tree, shed their larval casings, flex their wings, and enjoy a brief summer of winged activity. It is reported that newly hatched cicadas, deep fried, make a good coctail party tidbit, certainly a conversation piece.

Spiders and their Relations. These eight-legged artisans are intriguing, as everyone knows who has taken time to watch one. By manufacturing and cagily using the highest quality nets, spiders trap billions of insects every day. One authority says that the insects killed by the spiders of England and Wales in one year would weigh more than the total human population of those countries. Spiders kill their prey by poisonous bite but they seldom bite humans. When they do, the usual bite is no more annoying than that of a mosquito.

Of the many varieties of spiders in the United States only the black widow and the brown recluse have killed humans and only the females are dangerous. The black widow is a large, pea-sized spider with a red hour-glass design on the underside of her abdomen. Black widows principally inhabit dark moist places, as cellars and outhouses. While more common in the South and in California, this spider is widespread through the United States. Bed rest should be prescribed for any victim of a black widow bite. If the patient has hypertensive heart disease, bed rest is imperative. Ice packs or warm baths will ease muscle spasm pain and a physician may administer antivenin.

In 1957 the first documented case of serious injury from a brown recluse spider, *Loxosceles reclusus,* a Lower Midwest resident, was reported. This oval-bodied species, slightly smaller than the black widow,

Brown recluse

Black widow

varies from light fawn to dark chocolate in color and bears a violin-shaped black mark on the back of its head. The bite, which may occur in the open field as well as in the house, is usually mildly stinging or painless. Since fatal bites by this spider are on record, medical attention should be sought.

Mites. Mites, which are tiny relatives of the spiders, will move to a passerby from infested vegetation and leave numerous small, persistent, red bite marks on the skin. Some relief may be had by application of

Tick unengorged × 2

Mite × 50

Tick engorged × 2

camphorated phenol in mineral oil. This asphyxiates the mites and reduces the itching and pain. Mites are not considered dangerous though some persons will exhibit allergic reactions. Scabies, a mite-caused disease, is not one associated with outdoor living.

Ticks. These unattractive blood-sucking parasites are not insects, but remotely related to the spiders. They frequently infest brushlands where there are cattle or deer. Should you find one attached to you after a walk in the woods, do not try to pull it off, for the head may break off and cause infection. Apply a little alcohol or ammonia to its rear end and it will usually let go. Ticks can be carriers of serious diseases, among them spotted fever.

Sprays, Traps, and Repellents

Insecticide Spraying. Modern agriculture has become dependent on insecticide sprays, and chemical spraying has been so widely applied to other problems that now, as every person must know, much of our environment has become seriously polluted from the residues. This affects all forms of wildlife, and, more than is generally recognized, man. Whether the spraying is done with a hand-held pressure can, a tank truck, or spread by plane, the poisons become successively concentrated through the food chain until they reach us in meats and milk, and have even reached the animals of Antarctica.

In Connecticut DDT spraying against the gypsy moth killed birds, frogs and toads, salamanders, trout and other fish, beneficial insects, and other forms of life, including natural enemies of the gypsy moth. Numerous court actions have been taken by property owners to prevent insecticide spraying by plane. In one such case in New Jersey it was pointed out that in spraying against the gypsy moth 250,000 honey bees had also been killed. Biological controls, now developed for a few agricultural pests, are not of much help to the individual landowner.

Before undertaking any extensive spray campaign it is well to obtain latest advice from your regional agricultural agent and to check such advice with local conservation organizations. If you plan to use any sprays or foggers about your premises read the directions with care, follow their advice, and be moderate in your application. Leave no container or applicator of such poisons around where an illiterate but curious child could be exposed to it.

There are many sprays for many purposes. DDT, malathion, parathion, dieldrin, heptachlor, chlordane, and aldrin have become household words because of their wide use, but each is a poison to be used only with full understanding of the consequences and the alternates. Sevin is one brand that is less lethal to wildlife and has less persistent residues, but during a ten-day period after application it is rated as "very toxic."

Pyrethrum is a natural insecticide that does not have such persistent toxicity in soils as do the chlorinated hydrocarbons. It is also preferable to the ultra-powerful organo-phosphates. In reading the labels on insecticide containers you may find one with the active ingredient listed as pyrethrin. Hargate is such a product and though it will kill a wide variety of insects and spiders it may be safely used on the skin of most humans and warmblooded animals, though some persons will show allergic reactions. The sprays are toxic to fish. It is reported that insects do not develop immunity to this poison, as flies do to DDT. It is obtainable directly from Mylen Company, 230 East 25th Street, New York, N.Y. 10010.

Insect Traps and Electric Grids. Insect traps come in great variety, and as stated before are not always as useful as their catches would indicate. Japanese beetle traps are efficient and important and are best purchased from your garden supply store. Electrocuting traps are available in several models, including bird-cage lanterns and screens. The working element is a grid of heavy wires about one-quarter inch apart. They use little current. When insects, drawn by bait or light, fly between the charged wires, the moisture in their bodies causes the current to short-circuit and the insects are thus electrocuted. There is no danger to people as the screens are shielded. Some, but not all, insect traps use ultraviolet light effectively. The size of the catch of these killers is impressive, both with flies and moths, but they are not particularly selective and beneficial insects are destroyed along with those that are pests. As is true of other fly traps they may draw in insects from surrounding territory and will not necessarily leave your premises with a reduced population.

Yellow light bulbs provide suitable illumination for unscreened porches and patios without attracting as many insects as will a white light.

Insect Repellents. Both in liquid and in stick form repellents are effective. To what extent they build up toxins in the body apparently is not well known. Frequent use of such repellents should be avoided by anyone who is sensitive to them. Repellents in aerosol sprays should never be used near children, near the face, nor indeed anywhere that the fog could be breathed.

The U.S. Department of Agriculture has carried on extensive testing of insect repellents and findings indicate that products based on "deet" (diethyltoluamide) present the best combination of safety, effectiveness, and applicability to many species. Of the many repellents on the market *Off* is satisfactory, as is *Mosquitone,* both available in liquid form. The foam type is also acceptable.

Other Invertebrates. Earthworms? Nightcrawlers? They are important agents in aeration of the soil, and enrich it by pulling the green plant material on which they feed into their tunnels, thus enriching both themselves and the soil. If you are a bait fisherman and want a good supply of worms, maintain a compost pile into which earth is mixed. In the colder parts of New England some people keep a worm barrel in their basement over winter, tossing in a few vegetable trimmings, coffee grounds, orange skins, and other items to keep the worms content until spring when they may be put out to forage for themselves in the garden. This is supposed to give the garden an earlier start.

Slugs and Snails. Slugs are mollusks without shells. Their presence may be first observed by the slimy trails that indicate their passage. The animals themselves avoid the bright drying sun and are most likely to be seen in the summer months shortly after dawn before they have retreated to some damp moist place beneath a stone or board. They will feed on many a choice plant and may provoke you into using one of the commercial preparations that are compounded to eliminate slugs and their relatives the snails. Metaldehyde is an effective control agent.

Snails, though highly destructive in many warmer lands, are rarely a problem here. A few colonies of European land snails, the edible species, have become established in our area, but perhaps because our winters are too severe they do not appear to thrive.

Crayfish. Lawns near streams and lakes are sometimes "disfigured" by the little mud chimneys that surround the inch-wide tunnels of crayfishes. Such holes go vertically down to or near water level. From these retreats the animals emerge at night to forage. If you can catch them outside their burrows or fish them out, as some are reported to do, you can use them as a good table item. Europeans do. But if eliminating them is your problem it will be easiest to poison them. DDT baits are effective but a better technique is to put about ten drops of carbon disulfide into each hole, using an oil can or medicine dropper for the purpose, and then closing the hole by pressing the earth with your heel.

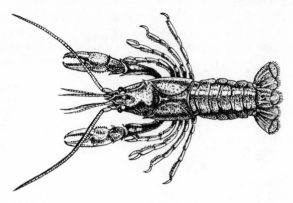

Crayfish

Caution! Carbon disulfide is highly inflammable and explosive. Do not smoke while applying it and avoid inhaling the fumes. A safer and less expensive crayfish poison is coal tar and creosote cattle dip, diluted 1 part to 150 parts of water. One or two ounces of this per burrow should suffice.

Swimmers' Itch. Swimmers' itch is the name for an irritation caused by a small water-dwelling parasite that may burrow into your skin to no lasting ill effect but to temporary discomfort. While you are in the water the invading animal is unable to penetrate the skin but in the moments after you emerge the parasite can push against the surface film of water and then you acquire the itch. If you towel thoroughly and quickly the parasite is defeated. Because the normal host for these parasites is a snail, areas that are infested may be treated with a molluscicide, a matter for state health authorities.

9. Community Affairs and Yours

About 35 of every 100 metropolitan fringe families change their residences every few years, some of them even three or four times in a working lifetime. Thus, many of our suburban residents have a sense of impermanence. They may send half a dozen children to the public schools and pay $1,000 a year in local taxes, but the transitory nature of their residence makes them feel unqualified for extensive public service.

Old-time residents stay in power, unconvinced of the need of adjusting to modern trends. Frequently the intransigence of long-time local residents postpones adjustment to modern influences until enough newcomers have swung the balance of power.

Studies at Pittsburgh, Pennsylvania, and Lansing, Michigan, revealed suburbs controlled by entrenched rural-minded leaders resistant to change. Zoning, new street lights, traffic control, and school problems were not their prime interests. Local government designed for the 19th century was not equipped to handle problems of the 1960s and '70s. Urban sprawl, auto graveyards, highway ribbon growth, low-grade housing, spotty development, commuter difficulties, and traffic congestion are weighty problems requiring weighty attention—the best that local, state and federal government can give them.

The final responsibility is the voter's. If he elects people who, through ignorance or design, oppose or sabotage a planned community, he bears the responsibility for the unplanned hodge-podge of urban sprawl that follows. People who want to have park lands or residential lands rezoned frequently have an interest in the result—a monetary interest. With the rapid disappearance of the limited resource of space, integrity in a local public official is more important than ever before.

One of the worst examples of local government action against the public interest occurred in suburban Washington, D.C., in November 1966. In less than four years the County Council of Montgomery County, Maryland, had rezoned 15 square miles. Then in the November 1966 election, the "Builders' Council," as it was known, was voted out of office. Before the new Council could take office, the "Builders' Council" resumed rezoning wildly. In its last two days in office, the Council rezoned more than 2,000 acres. This action opened the door for commercial and industrial development, townhouses and apartments.

But the results were more far-reaching than this. Rock Creek, which flows from Maryland through the District of Columbia and into the Potomac, has part of its watershed in Montgomery County. Federal agencies were cooperating in long-range planning for Rock Creek. When the lame duck Council rezoned watershed lands, the Soil Conservation Service of the U.S. Department of Agriculture promptly withdrew $500,000 in funds allotted to the county.

The Interior Department predicted that, as a result of the rezoning, "Rock Creek is going to end up as a dirty trickle subject to occasional flash floods rolling tons of silt down to the Potomac estuary and sorely endangering prospects for the restoration of that body of water as well. Widespread construction of pavements, parking lots and rooftops has diminished Rock Creek's flow."

The new Council fortunately was able to undo most of the damage wrought by its predecessor. Suburban dwellers interested in an attractive, healthy environment can cure many of their woes at the ballot box.

The courts have supported the use of state and federal action to bring about a well-ordered community. The U.S. Supreme Court said in 1954, "It is within the power of the legislature to determine that the community should be beautiful as well as healthy, spacious as well as clean, well-balanced as well as carefully patrolled."

Congress has authorized a Land and Water Conservation Fund, 60 percent apportioned on a 50–50 matching basis to help the states and local communities acquire and develop park and recreation areas, the other 40 percent for the acquisition of federal recreation areas. In 1965 Congress authorized the Department of Housing and Urban Development to make 50 percent matching grants to communities acquiring lands for permanent public recreation and scenic use.

Under the Cropland Adjustment Program of the Department of Agriculture, federal funds for acquiring green space were made available to urban areas. States and local governments wanting to buy cropland for conservation purposes, to facilitate pollution control, or for wildlife habitat and recreation have been provided with CAP grants as part of a "Greenspan" plan.

Parks, playgrounds, and reservoirs are also supportable uses. The Secretary of Agriculture has been authorized to pay part of the costs necessary to assure protection of the land in its new use.

Many suburbs find it necessary to set up special districts to protect certain areas or provide specific services: districts for sewage disposal, water supply, flood protection, parks and open space, recreation, and resource conservation. Such districts answer the need for coping with problems neither urban nor rural. In some areas, groups of citizens, banding together in non-governmental units, achieve similar ends.

By what legal means can governmental authority influence land use? Some of the more practical devices are tax inducements through graduated rates, exemptions or deferment; government aid in cash, materials or services to encourage soil or water conservation; zoning; land acquisition by purchase, gift or condemnation, or through reversion for non-payment of taxes.

The following notes on related matters in some of the states covered by this book are not intended to be comprehensive but cite some significant efforts. Many equally commendable examples are taking place in other states:

In Connecticut, conservation commissions were authorized in 1961, patterned after a pioneering Massachusetts model. About half of the state's towns now have such commissions.

The Cook County, Illinois, Forest Preserve District was organized in 1915 and is one of the oldest designed to preserve forest lands on the county level.

In Iowa, conservation boards have been given power to levy an annual property tax for acquisition of public parks and conservation areas.

Kentucky's junkyard law requires junkyard owners to screen scrapped car yards from public view, and this brought compliance by 75 percent of the state's 758 junk dealers in the first 13 months of enforcement. Another 800 locations were cleaned up and removed from the junkyard category. Screening by fences, trees, hedges, shrubs or other foliage is considered acceptable.

In Massachusetts, the need for organized local action to meet conservation needs led to passage of legislation in 1957 providing for conservation commissions at town or municipal level. State aid for land acquisition was provided in later legislation. By 1965, 240 of the state's 351 towns each had a conservation commission of three to seven members.

The commissions have been reflecting a growing concern for the total environment, rather than stressing an isolated problem or eyesore. Four of their major objectives have been: wildlife habitat preservation, inclusion of conservation in making community master plans, adequate recreation areas, and elimination of water pollution.

Some 200 projects costing slightly less than $1 million were under way in 1965. The state's 15 soil and water conservation districts assist the local communities as well as landowners, making soil studies and soil maps to ascertain the best sites for residential and industrial use—schools, highways, parks, forests and playgrounds.

In Michigan, the area with the largest urban fringe is the Detroit-Dearborn-Pontiac megalopolis. It provides in some degree for its open space needs through a special governmental unit. A five-county agency, the Huron-Clinton Metropolitan Authority, was formed in 1940 by popular vote to provide parks and recreational facilities along the Huron and Clinton rivers. In 1964 the Authority opened the latest of eight parks, which range from 4,300 to 115 acres. Parkways are also set up by the Authority, which assesses a one-quarter mill property tax on the assessed valuation of the member counties. The Authority allows no hunting, removal of plant life, or interference with bird and animal life. Nature trails and programs are provided, and some of the parks have naturalists on the payroll. With a few exceptions, all facilities are free.

The park areas which help to make life tolerable for New York City's suburbanites operate under a wide range of authority. National, inter-state, county and local agencies operate conservation and recreation areas surrounding New York City on the east, north and northwest. These facilities range from Fire Island National Seashore, off the south shore of Long Island, to Palisades Interstate Park on the west side of the Hudson River northwest of the city. Long Island has a dozen state parks ranging from 1,755 to 97 acres. Westchester County, north of the city, has another dozen or so, ranging from 4,270 acres to 30.

Palisades Interstate Park is probably the best known of these green acre treasures. Its 55,154 acres are controlled by a Palisades Interstate Park Commission of ten members from New York and New Jersey. The Palisades protection movement began early in the century when the great basaltic cliffs along the Hudson were being chipped and dynamited away by rock quarry companies.

Several private agencies also play a large part in the saving of park lands in New York. Among them is the Open Space Action Committee, cited in the Introduction, which launched its drive for suburban greenbelts in December 1965 with publication of a book, *Stewardship*. Designed to encourage a sense of responsibility for the land on the part of landowner, community, and civic leaders, the book was given wide distribution in New York City's 16 suburban counties, contiguous but lying in three states.

The refreshing aspect of this program is its pragmatic approach. Well financed, the Committee can back up its well-worded preachments with action. It offers model ordinances for cluster communities, and plans for tax relief for landowners who agree not to bulldoze their property. It encourages land donations to municipalities and conservation groups. The Committee comprises representatives from powerful conservation organizations, some of whose members are affluent landowners. This fact conceivably could help the Committee in achieving the practical goals of its imaginative concept.

The Western Pennsylvania Conservancy is a volunteer conservation action group that grew from less than 50 members in 1958 to 6,500 in 1966. It has acquired and sold to the state more than 14,000 acres for state park and other conservation use. The Conservancy administers nature reserves, hiking trails, and guided tours for conservation education.

The Pennsylvania Roadside Council has led the fight against billboards, auto junkyards, and highway ugliness for many years. It has set high standards for scenic highways. Its engineers prepared an impressive model of an ideal expressway, tailored to fit into the scenic landscape.

Rhode Island, the smallest state, followed Massachusetts' example in 1960 and authorized establishment of Conservation Commissions. Half of the state's towns had commissions by 1966. Vermont enacted legislation authorizing Conservation Commissions in 1965.

The state of Wisconsin began a ten-year program in the early 1960s designed to preserve open space and provide recreation facilities. Local governments are authorized to buy land. The $50 million plan, supported by a special tax on cigarettes, calls for extensive land purchases; but public easements will be taken on large areas of highway scenic resources, wildlife habitat, and park and forest areas. By acquiring conservation rights, Wisconsin expects to preserve natural beauty along roads, parkways and water bodies; protect entrances to state parks; preserve fish and wildlife habitat; facilitate stream bank improvement and water control.

Landscaping

Any community interested in having an attractive landscape and a pleasing, healthful environment will have its own landscape architect. His role could be as vital as the mayor's, if not more so. Yet, how many communities today have such planners? Billions of dollars worth of highway construction are completed without the advice of trained specialists in plant life, wildlife, ecological principles, and interrelated terrain and environmental factors. H. F. Werkmeister, a German landscape architect specializing in saving destroyed landscapes, observes that time has almost run out for a systematic effort to save the natural landscape in many countries.

Green spaces are as indispensable to the public good, says Jean-Bernard Perrin, head of the Green Spaces Services of Paris, as food or drinking water. Mass housing projects around Paris have aroused so much concern over their dreary sameness that the French government approved a master plan to save the countryside. The plan authorized drastic measures to set up a belt of 500,000 hectares of landscapes, woods, forests, water courses, and villages. The state also could take over a number of private forests averaging 10,000 hectares. It could even stipulate the nature and shape of bridges, barns, water towers, gas containers, and transformers. Power lines were to be placed within special lanes in the interior of the zone. Industrial construction was prohibited. Setbacks were required for buildings along arterial roads;

3,000 hectares of belts along the arterial roads were kept free of buildings.

Nature Centers

Open spaces suitable for hiking and nature study are essential adjuncts of a metropolitan area and should be incorporated in the planning of any community: urban, suburban, or rural. A good nature center consists of natural land and vegetation, simple trails with natural history information on labels, and a structure of some sort in which there can be reference books and other facilities promoting the group study of the natural environment. Many secondary schools now incorporate simple natural areas in their planning. Prominent as an aid to planning is the Nature Centers Division of the National Audubon Society.

By the fall of 1966, NCD had taken part in the planning of nature centers in 200 cities. At least 55 centers were in full operation and the remainder were in various stages of development. The division stresses educational as well as recreational values and has definite ideas on what a nature center should be—a minimum of 50 acres is required, for example. Nature clubs or the local Audubon society often find the tracts that are best suited for nature center use. If the property is owned by private enterprise, a company may want to donate the land or sell it at a nominal fee. Other private enterprise may be enlisted to help in raising the necessary funds. Garden clubs, churches, men's service clubs have sponsored nature trails, buildings and equipment. Some successful nature center ventures in the East and Midwest are the following:

In Peoria, Illinois, a non-profit group turned over 491 wooded acres to a park district to assure preservation of plant and animal life, an "outdoor laboratory," a recreation site for hiking, photography and similar nature hobbies, library and museum space, and meeting areas for nature groups. By 1961 the Forest Park Wildlife Refuge and Nature Education Center had 3 ½ miles of nature trails, nature classes, nature tours, hikes and talks. Picnicking, horseback riding, camping and shooting are not allowed.

In Nebraska, the publisher of the *Lincoln Journal* proposed a 40-acre memorial and contributed $3,000. The city park board and Lincoln Audubon Naturalist Society gave a hand and the Chet Ager Bird and Wildlife Study Center was dedicated in May 1963. The center has woods, walkways, a museum, abundant animal life, two lakes, a marsh and open land. Observation points encourage photography, and plant and wildlife study.

A spectacular nature center at Kalamazoo, Michigan, contains a 300-

acre preserve of wooded, rolling land and a $750,000 interpretive building. Dedicated in October 1964, it provides classes for children, a program of natural resources management, and demonstration facilities along several miles of trails. Pets, radios, littering, trampling, picnicking, camping, hunting, fishing, trapping, and building fires are prohibited.

Nationwide, about 35 new nature centers, including seasonal centers, are being opened a year. While some are in state parks and similar lands, the bulk of the centers benefit urban and suburban areas. Assuming that the average center covers about 100 acres, at least 200,000 acres of open space will have been saved around our expanding cities and suburbs by the year 2000.

"This amount of breathing space is certain to have beneficial effects on the patterns of land use in urban and suburban areas," says Dr. Joseph J. Shomon, NCD director. "It is not the quantity of open space that is important but the quality and where and how we save and use it."

These 200,000 acres may not seem overwhelming, but when carefully parceled in small 100-acre tracts around 2,000 cities, they can spell the difference between a megalopolitan nightmare and a well-planned, green-carpeted America.

Highways

A new expressway invariably changes some suburban living habits. To reach a school formerly a half-mile away, you now may have to drive three miles by overpass. The character of the community may change, too—for the worse if the highway uses up park land, for the better if it wipes out blighted areas. Whether the freeway, beltway or expressway is within sight of your house or ten miles away, it will channel more people in your direction. The result is larger suburbs accompanied by commercial establishments and the personnel to maintain them. It also means the loss of the country and wildlands in which to roam.

Just as the railroads did much to set the pattern of the nation's westward growth in the 19th century, today's new highways are helping to determine the formation and location of suburban population centers. The expressway planners remodel our landscape and social structure. "Our future patterns of land use will be based on that of our growing highway system as surely as the human body is molded about its skeleton," notes conservationist Paul B. Sears.

The traumatic effect of a new freeway on a landowner or a community may be greatly softened through state or local governmental action. In Iowa, for example, if you are a landowner and your property is in the path of a highway interchange, the state highway commission will arrange a land exchange for you. You swap your property, now earmarked for an interchange, for land of equal value and character. Iowa has authorized its highway commission to buy and sell lands for this purpose. It affords little comfort, however, if one has invested time and affection in a property.

In Wisconsin and some other states, if your property is wanted for a highway route, the law requires that the state pay you a fair amount *before* you give up possession. Legislation authorizing such payments, including moving expenses, is needed in many states.

There is ample evidence that many state highway programs are being pushed to completion with little regard to the effects on the surrounding suburbs and countryside. Gasoline taxes are bringing state highway authorities a golden bonanza. In the sometimes dim world of state and county politics, juicy construction contracts and political allegiance are to some degree intertwined. Because gasoline taxes are usually earmarked for highway use, new highways must be built, though wondering taxpayers might prefer a different use, or at least a different route than that chosen.

Conservation minded people are especially aware of highway activities because of the continual pressure to take parks and other relatively unspoiled areas for highway routes. Few of our major cities have escaped controversy in some suburban area over proposals to force a highway through a woods, or over plans to widen a tree-canopied roadway. In many cases the new or improved road offers less lasting value to the community than the tree-lined lane, untrammeled shore, or wooded ridge slope it would replace.

Some communities have been successful in resisting questionable highway schemes about to be inflicted on their lands rich in scenic or historical values. In Danvers, Massachusetts, for example, the citizens diverted an interstate highway and forestalled a 200-unit real estate subdivision. The town valued its historic character and open spaces so highly that it raised a $300,000 bond issue to finance the necessary land arrangements.

In opposing county and local government officials on certain freeway routes, a community needs and expects advice. Here again the Soil Conservation Service, through its National Soil Survey, can provide information for the asking on the advantages and limitations of proposed routes in respect to comparative soils, water, and drainage problems.

Effects on Property Values

Between 1946 and 1966 about 60 studies were made of urban, suburban, and small town land values as affected by major highways. Most of the studies show that property values have either increased or have remained unchanged. Residential values are no exception.

Along the Route 60 expressway at Lawrenceville, Illinois, one-family developments have thrived. Land values rose nine times higher in the 18 years after the highway was built. Similar land on a secondary road rose only 1.5 times in value.

Residential values within half a mile of the Edens Expressway in Illinois have increased faster than values for all properties farther removed. At Lexington, Massachusetts, residential land values near Route 128 have risen more than twice as fast as values of land elsewhere in the area. Values of property along the Penn Lincoln Parkway at Monroeville, Pennsylvania, rose 336 percent after completion of the parkway in 1953. Values of similar land not on the parkway rose only 74 percent.

The U.S. Bureau of Public Roads says: "Owners of property adjacent to improved highways generally benefit greatly in terms of land value gains. Improved highways, expressways in particular, exert a very favorable influence on urban and suburban property values in general."

Even when a local government loses property producing substantial taxes, the net result may be a gain. Frederick County, Maryland, lost $550,000 in assessments when U.S. 40 and U.S. 240 took over a right-of-way, but the county's general property tax base rose by $47.5 million in the ensuing ten years. Tarrytown, New York, lost $700,000 worth of property to the New York Thruway but soon had new assessments of $1 million and almost $50 million worth of new or proposed construction.

Dollar value, of course, does not necessarily reflect the actual value of the land to the country, or even to the local community. An uncultivated meadow or a swamp, with its wildlife, flowers, trees, and intricate ecology, may offer values far more significant than the dollar values attached to a subdivision lot, however "well-located" it may be.

Residents of suburban Westchester County, New York, battled for five years over two possible routes for Interstate Highway 87. In April 1966 the Federal Highway administrator finally chose the more scenic route. The donor of an affected wildlife sanctuary said she would close the refuge. *The New York Times* called the administrator's decision "disastrous to one of the last remaining sections of unspoiled natural beauty in the metropolitan area . . . another needless triumph over woodland and meadow." The government claimed that the chosen route was $4.3 billion cheaper and argued that the motorist deserves striking vistas. This led the *Times* to question whether a steady stream of carbon-monoxide-producing automobiles enhances natural beauty.

The Federal Bureau of Public Roads found that "most modern highways are acceptable to the major portion of residents in the areas that they serve." Attitudes were checked in New York, Massachusetts, Michigan, Maryland, California and Texas. Californians and Texans were heavily in favor of new, modern highways.

Many suburban communities are finding that modern highways attract both new residents and choice industries. Smokestack factories are giving way to garden type industrial parks. The tax burden is thus broadened as well as increased.

A new major highway also may stimulate a community and set it to thinking—and planning. The number of towns near the Connecticut Turnpike with planning commissions increased from 5 in 1955–56 to 10 in 1957–58. Zoning commission towns increased from 6 to 12. Outside of the highway's influence, only one town added a planning commision.

Highway planners and suburban planners are frequently teaming up for community betterment. Slums and other blighted areas then give way to the right-of-way, but there is, as yet, little concern for the families so displaced. The suburbs rarely welcome the unhoused people and so new slums are created.

Roadside Planting

A highway without ample setbacks, and trees and shrubs (whether natural or planted) is a bore rather than a boon. Since 1944 garden clubs have been beautifying a national system of "blue star memorial highways" extending some 25,000 miles. These efforts have probably saved many lives as well as the roadside landscape. Studies show that trees, shrubs and grass pay dividends in lives and dollars as well as in visual appeal. Vegetation controls highway shoulder and bank erosion, reduces the snowdrift hazard, modifies headlight glare, and reduces deadly monotony. Heavy hedges such as multiflora rose help prevent collisions and roadside cliff plunges. From the community's viewpoint, hedges, trees and shrubs muffle highway noise, conceal speeding traffic, and provide a touch of green to the environment.

Billboard Blight

The attractiveness of a suburban community is usually in inverse ratio to the number of its advertising signs. Those with landscaped roadways and deep setbacks, with their neatness and scenic charm, attract residents whose values may be your own.

The automobile has remade much of the American landscape but it hasn't done a very good job of it. By the mid-1930s the 47-mile road between Newark and Trenton, New Jersey, was lined with 472 billboards, 300 gasoline stations, 440 other commercial users, and 165 intersections. This averaged out to 16 commercial users, 6 gas stations, 3.5 intersections and 10 billboards per mile.

This roadside defacement was bad enough but today on many highways it is even worse. Ten billboards per mile would be a low score on some roads. If creatures from outer space suddenly landed and littered up our countryside with signs the size of boxcars we would resist it as a gross indignity to our natural environment. Yet the outdoor advertising industry has been getting away with a similar activity since the 19th century. Hawaii is perhaps our most beautiful state, kept so in part by prohibiting billboards. Vermont recently enacted a similar law.

Few, if any, other fields of enterprise can match the outdoor advertisers for brash irresponsibility to the public welfare. They commandeer the road user's field of vision and expropriate his attention. Whether or not they rent the billboard sites, they boldly exploit a public thoroughfare for a purpose for which it was not constructed. They are taking from you something they do not own—your field of vision. The advertisers arrogate a right they have not been given and qualifications they do not possess.

Outdoor advertising, by commanding the motorist's attention, distracts the driver and increases the accident rate. Some intersections having four or more signs had an average accident rate approximately three times that for signless intersections.

The citizens of Oregon discovered the power of positive billboard thinking when it attempted to put through some "visual litter" reforms. Disgusted at their legislature's long subservience to billboard pressures, civic-minded groups succeeded in obtaining a referendum on billboard control. In the first two months of the referendum campaign, the billboard firms inundated the state with leaflets screaming that the state's $176,000,000 tourist industry would suffer due to loss of signboards telling tourists where to eat and sleep. The Highway Protection Committee spent $10,000 advocating billboard control; the advertising forces spent $107,967 advocating billboards—and won. It was a Pyrrhic victory, however. Oregon billboard foes regrouped and the state eventually adopted billboard controls. Other states have not been so successful.

In 1958 Congress passed the Federal-aid Highway Act to control outdoor advertising on the National System of Interstate and Defense Highways. A state's compliance would be rewarded with an extra one-half of one percent of the federal contribution toward the cost of interstate highways within the state. Yet by 1966 only 20 of the 44 states considering legislation on this question had authorized billboard controls on their portions of the interstate highway.

At the White House Conference on Natural Beauty in May 1965, the Roadside Control panel recommended legislation requiring states to spend at least three percent of their federal-aid highway funds for scenic beauty purposes. The panel also recommended that no funds be allotted to a state unless billboards were barred within 1,000 feet of the federal-state highway system and unless states prohibited automobile graveyards visible from such highways. Existing auto junkyards containing the rusting hulks of some 20 to 40 million cars were to be removed or screened. Senator Paul H. Douglas of Illinois went further. He suggested legislation in June 1966 that would require every car sold to "carry with it funds for its own burial."

By the time the outdoor advertising industry and the business-as-usual advocates finished lobbying in Washington, the proposed highway beautification legislation was but a shadow of the original plan. The billboard buffer zone had been whittled down from 1,000 to 660 feet, and there was to be no ban on billboards in areas zoned for commerce or business.

Public Utilities

Overhead power and telephone lines mar the attractiveness of many suburbs. Why, suburban residents ask, don't the power and telephone companies provide underground installations in the suburbs as they have done in urban centers? The answer: (1) high costs and (2) lack of public demand.

Without group action, the average landowner may find it costly and difficult to keep his property out of the shadow of power and telephone lines. For several hundred dollars he probably could have the telephone and power companies run their lines into his house underground. But this still wouldn't eliminate the poles and wires in adjacent roadways, and the wires running to his neighbors' houses.

The outlook is not hopeless, however, if the landowners in the neighborhood are all desirous of eliminating overhead wiring. Some 78 percent of the country's major utilities were willing to provide underground wiring in new housing subdivisions as long ago as 1960, if the developer would pay the added costs. Obviously, if the landowners will pick up the tab, the utilities will put their wires underground. Maintenance costs decrease in relation to storm interruption of service and injury from high power wires, though interruptions brought about by careless power shovel operators prove equally costly.

Some telephone companies offer underground wiring because of lower maintenance costs. In Seattle, Washington, one residential community formed a local improvement district to put utility lines underground. The landowners each paid $1,000 and the utility company put up another $300 per house. Costs of undergrounding depend largely on the soil, the ease of digging, and the power consumption the utility can expect. Buried power cables are more costly than those used overhead.

The legislature might require utilities to place at least portions of their lines underground as a condition of their franchise. The legislation could allow a rate increase to pay half of the costs. Swifter action, however, is more likely in local communities where the use of public highways and streets by utilities is not a divine right. Utility poles and wires are there by sufferance of the community, and the courts have upheld the right of communities to charge public utilities for the use of community streets. A 1961 study showed that it would cost suburban utilities $22.2 million if they had to quit their public property routes and acquire private easements.

The local community, then, is in a position to demand certain installation conditions if it is to permit the utility to use its streets. Tax abatement is another incentive which the community can offer for favorable action on suggestions to "go underground."

Help to suburbia may be on the way, however. In May 1966 a U.S. Senate committee was mulling over the prospect of 20 million acres being creased and slashed by power line right-of-ways by 1980. The acreage devoted to a parade of towers and wires across the countryside would be nearly twice that in our present national park system. The committee was considering a bill that would offer power companies tax credits for underground wiring, and that called for federal research on the power line problem.

Pollution Fees or Penalties?

Air and water pollution are now a major concern of many suburban communities. How to bar or control contamination practices which have prevailed for a century is causing some governmental dilemmas on the local level. Cultivating a sense of community responsibility among individuals, private enterprise and municipalities is the obvious goal, but usually tougher, faster action is needed.

Strict enforcement of anti-contamination ordinances, with heavy fines and the social stigma of jail sentences, is considered the most effective method. Experts on air and water pollution take a dim view of proposals which would allow polluters to pay a regular, legal fee for polluting the air or waters. Fees would cloak polluters with legality and encourage delays in cleanup efforts. Tax relief to offset the cost of pollution abatement equipment, however, offers an attractive inducement.

There are specific practices which the homeowner may follow to avoid unduly contributing to air and water pollution. In a well organized community such practices will be obligatory.

In septic tank communities the tank must be regularly emptied and cleaned; the effluent not allowed to flow into a stream or lake without first being cleaned by distribution through an efficient filter bed. In many lakeside summer colonies raw sewage is emptied directly into the waters, an act which in our time can be considered but criminal.

In lines connected with public sewer systems the use of sink-connected garbage disposals, convenient and economical though they may be, contributes enormously to the load of municipal disposal systems and, in turn, to the pollution of waters through overloading them with nitrates. Few sewage disposal plants are engineered to meet the heavy loads imposed upon them.

The modern bio-degradable detergents, used both domestically and commercially, are not as bad as those used a few years ago which capped many rivers with foam, detergents which by public concern were forced off the market. But further improvements are called for.

Air pollution will be lessened if you do not burn trash, but send it out for burial. The autumn downfall of leaves, instead of being burned may in part be used as winter cover for the garden, or totally converted to compost by establishing a bin or corner of the garden into which all plant material can be tossed to rot.

Be certain, too, that your house warming system is working efficiently, with complete combustion of the fuel. Gas fired furnaces contribute less to air pollution than do those burning oil or coal.

Law and Wildlife

Vertebrate animals (mammals, birds, reptiles, amphibians, and fish) for the greater part are considered public property though there are many of the smaller species which, uninteresting to the hunter, fisherman, or bird watcher, receive no degree of protection. Some predators that in fact or in theory have been thought inimicable to man's interests have been subject to destruction by government agents. The payment of bounties, thoroughly demonstrated as ineffective and economically unsound, still is practiced in some states but should everywhere be stopped.

Plant life, and most invertebrate animals (exceptions are species of commercial value) belong to the landowner. The extent of wildlife protection varies with species and state, but in general the protection is as follows: Migratory birds are protected by a treaty between the United States and Canada signed in 1916. This "Convention Between the United States and Great Britain for the Protection of Migratory Birds in the United States and Canada" afforded, for the first time, international protection to named migratory and non-game birds. (A similar treaty with Mexico was signed in 1936.) The treaty protects nine families of migratory game birds and 33 families of insectivorous and other non-game species. (For hawks and owls, see below.) Ducks, geese, mourning doves, rails, snipe and woodcock are protected except during state hunting seasons.

House sparrows, crows, and starlings flourish despite widespread non-protection by the states. Michigan also exempts blackbirds from protection. "Blackbirds" can cover a number of species, including starlings, grackles and blackbirds. Connecticut protects blackbirds but allows reprisals on offending red-wings and crows if the birds are destroying corn.

Most states protect wild turkey, bobwhite quail, ruffed grouse, prairie chicken and ringnecked pheasant except during a hunting season.

It is illegal to remove, destroy or possess nests, eggs or nestlings of migratory species at any time of year without permits (state and federal).

The capture and confinement of migratory songbirds is illegal. Some states (Maryland, for example) allow confinement of mammals and resident birds for a license fee. Retaining wild animals as pets, however, is not recommended; the animals are better off in the wild. Tender fawns, raised to adulthood, have been known to injure their benefactors with flailing hooves; carnivores may bite.

It's advisable to get copies of your state and local game laws every year and familiarize yourself with them. The average suburbanite may not be interested in shooting or trapping, but it helps the community if you can report out-of-season or other illegal taking of wildlife. You should know where your state stands on hawk and owl shooting.

Controlling the Trespasser

Signs saying "No Trespassing" lack the authority of those saying "No Trespassing, Under Full Penalty of the Law." A sign indicating that one is unwelcome is effective with most persons but there are always a few people who have to be convinced that the sign means what it says. Check your state regulations on posting. In some places you are not protected unless the signs bear your name, are annually renewed, and are posted at specified intervals around the property.

Trespassing—the unlawful entrance on the property of another person—is punishable in civil courts, and damages may be recovered by the property owner through civil action. Failure to see "No Trespassing" signs is no excuse; in fact, such failure is an unlawful act in itself. Yet a trespasser may sue you for injury received on your land.

The well-run suburb of today will not tolerate outright trespassing by strangers. Periodic police patrols and spot checks are effective. Cessation of milk and newspaper deliveries during the homeowner's out-of-town trips helps the police and makes the vacant home less conspicuous. Consult your local trespass laws. If a gun-carrying hunter or two cuts across your property, don't lodge a prolonged protest. Some landowners have been shot. If the trespasser doesn't move readily at your first request, call the police.

Appendix A.
Where to Find Advice, Help, and Material

There are many organizations, national to local, private and governmental, to which you may turn for help on your personal problems of land management, or on the desires of your community for its betterment. Government agencies are established to assist you with your problems of soil, water, preservation of open space, trees, animal life, pests, pollution, and the appearance of your access roadways. On occasion you may have reason to contact the central governmental offices in

Washington, but, for the greater part, assistance should first be sought at the local level. County Extension Agents from your Land Grant college, Soil Conservation Districts, state or county health officers, game wardens, all will be near at hand. The Federal offices in Washington cannot be expected to provide much more direct help to an individual than to provide appropriate printed matter. Appendix B of this book will give you quicker access to some of the publications pertinent to the matters previously discussed.

There are some 900 conservation agencies or other organizations seriously concerned with natural resource or natural beauty questions, problems, and goals. To help people find their way in this otherwise uncharted field of national, international, interstate, regional, state, and territorial groups, the National Wildlife Federation publishes a superb annual *Conservation Directory*. This is one of the most helpful publications available for anyone concerned with natural resources, whether it's shade tree problems in your yard or the plight of the Arabian oryx. The *Directory* contains the names and addresses of thousands of officials and other individuals in conservation as well as the names and addresses of the 900-plus agencies and organizations.

Another helpful publication, but solely for information about federal agencies, is the *United States Government Organization Manual,* published annually.

For published materials relating to nature, conservation, and the suburbs, two publications of the Reference Services, U. S. Department of the Interior, are prolific source guides. "Readings on the Preservation of Natural Beauty, August 1964" (mimeographed); and "Indexing and Abstracting Services," 1965, are both free at the department library, 18th and C Streets, N. W., Washington, D. C. 20240. "A Directory of Private Organizations Providing Assistance in Outdoor Recreation," and a little handbook "Federal Assistance in Outdoor Recreation . . ." listed below will also prove good guides to the many organizations with interests in the natural resources and their enjoyment.

Directories

Conservation Directory, 1967. A listing of organizations and officials concerned with natural resource use and management. National Wildlife Federation, 1412 16th Street, Washington 20036. 122 pages. $2.00

A Directory of Private Organizations Providing Assistance in Outdoor Recreation to Individuals, Organizations, Public Groups. Bureau of

Outdoor Recreation, U. S. Department of the Interior, Washington 20240. 1966. 74 pages. $.30. A directory oriented towards playtime.

Federal Assistance in Outdoor Recreation, Available to States, their Subdivisions, Organizations, Individuals. Bureau of Outdoor Recreation. 1966. 84 pages. $.35.

United States Government Organizational Manual. Office of the Federal Register, National Archives and Records Service, General Services Administration, Washington 20408. 783 pages. $1.75

Major Federal, State and Regional Agencies Helpful at the Rural Fringe

U.S. Department of Agriculture

Soil Conservation Service, Washington 20250. Through the Soil Conservation Districts it will give on-site technical assistance to landowners in developing, applying, and maintaining sound conservation plans on their land. Such planning may include consideration of land use, erosion control, woodland conservation, water, plant, and wildlife resources. The Service is concerned with pollution abatement because sediment from erosion is one of the leading pollutants of streams, rivers and lakes. Its staffs at state level may include biologists and conservationists, as well as soil experts. Some 3,000 conservation districts, originally intended to aid farmers, are units of state governments. They are now equipped to help suburban home owners, developers, urban fringe and rural residents. They issue government publications on planning, open land preserves, parks, roads and sewage systems; conduct workshops for town planners, consultants, businessmen and industrialists. Consult your phone book or county extension agent.

Agricultural Stabilization and Conservation Service

Its land use aid affects many urban fringe areas. Project costs may be shared with owners. Local offices are often found in your telephone book.

Forest Service, Washington 20250

Makes grants-in-aid for state and private forestry activities, and aids in area development. Persons with woodlots or tree plantations will find its publications helpful.

Agricultural Experiment Stations and Cooperative Extension Services

With Department of Agriculture support, Agricultural Experiment Stations are maintained for research at Land Grant colleges in each of the states. They work closely with the Federal Extension Services which are established at the same colleges. County Extension Agents are located in almost every county and it is to these that one turns first for help.

The state experiment station addresses are below. Except as otherwise stated address Agricultural Experiment Station:

Connecticut: Connecticut Agricultural Experiment Station, P. O. Box 1106, New Haven 06504. Also Storrs 06268

Delaware: Agricultural Experiment Station, University of Delaware, Newark 19711

Illinois: Urbana 61843

Indiana: Purdue University Agricultural Experiment Station, Lafayette 47907

Iowa: Agricultural Extension Service, Ames 50010

Kansas: Kansas State University Agricultural Experiment Station, Manhattan 66502

Kentucky: Lexington 40506

Maine: Maine Cooperative Extension Service, Orono 04473

Maryland: College Park 20742

Massachusetts: Cooperative Extension Service, University of Massachusetts, Amherst 01003

Michigan: Michigan State University Cooperative Extension Service, East Lansing 48823

Minnesota: University of Minnesota Agricultural Experiment Station, St. Paul 55101

Missouri: Columbia 65202

New Hampshire: Durham 03824

New Jersey: Rutgers Agricultural Experiment Station, New Brunswick 08903

New York: Agricultural Research Service, Ithaca 14850. Also Geneva 14456

Ohio: Ohio Agricultural Research and Development Center, Wooster 44691

Pennsylvania: Agricultural and Home Economics Extension Service, 108 Armsby Building, University Park 16802

Rhode Island: University of Rhode Island Agricultural Experiment Station, Kingston 02881

Tennessee: Knoxville 37900

Vermont: Burlington 05401

West Virginia: West Virginia University Agricultural Experiment Station, Morgantown 26506

Wisconsin: Madison 53706

U.S. Department of the Interior, Washington 20240

Bureau of Sports Fisheries and Wildlife. Its publications and authority concern the environment of wildlife, including game fishes. Migratory birds and national wildlife refuges are in its charge.

Bureau of Outdoor Recreation. It is authorized to provide technical assistance and to cooperate with the states, their political subdivisions, and private interests, in relation to outdoor recreation.

U.S. Department of Transportation, Washington 20235

Bureau of Public Roads. As administrators of the Highway Beautification Act of 1965, the Bureau is in a position to advise on and encourage the improvement in appearance of highways.

U.S. Department of Housing and Urban Development

Office for Metropolitan Development, Washington 20410. Printed matter and assistance is available on *urban* open space and beautification.

Regional offices of HUD in this area are the following:

Northeast States: Public Affairs Office, 346 Broadway, New York City 10013. *Middle Atlantic States, District of Columbia, and West Virginia:* 728 Weidener Building, Philadelphia, Pa. 19017. *North Central States:* Metropolitan Development Office, Room 1200, 360 North Michigan Ave., Chicago, Ill. 60601. *Kentucky and Tennessee:* 645 Peachtree-Seventh Building, Atlanta, Ga. 30323. *Missouri and Kansas:* 819 Taylor Street Ft. Worth, Texas 76102.

U.S. Department of Defense

Army Corps of Engineers, Washington 20315. It will answer inquiries about beach erosion and corrective construction and under some conditions can pay up to 70 per cent of the cost. It also will prepare flood plain studies.

General Services Administration, Washington 20405

The GSA will provide information concerning surplus federal lands disposable to state or local units for conservation or similar use.

133

Tennessee Valley Authority, Knoxville, Tennessee. Within its area
it will provide information on flood prevention measures, watershed
usage, and recreation development to organized groups.

State Agencies

Your state has agencies equipped to give aid and information on
conservation matters ranging from ducks to detergents. Whether
they are conservation commissions, agriculture departments, health
departments or highway bureaus, these agencies can provide you
valuable advice and possibly financial aid in solving individual or
community conservation problems. Consult your telephone book or
call your county Extension Service Agent.

State Universities

Most states provide short courses and informational materials on
land use and zoning through the state universities. Request a listing
from your nearest university.

Private Organizations, National

The Garden Club of America, 598 Madison Avenue, New York City
10022. It is available for assistance on local land acquisition projects
for open space and parklands. It serves to stimulate personal action
in conservation affairs. It annually distributes packets, "The World
Around You," to teachers and leaders in conservation.

American Society of Planning Officials, 1313 East 60th Street, Chicago 60637. Can guide one to consulting services.

Conservation Law Society of America, 1500 Mills Tower, 220 Bush
Street, San Francisco 94104. Its purpose is to provide legal aid on a
fee basis in relation to highway and other encroachment on parks.

National Recreation and Park Assoc., 1700 Pennsylvania Ave., N.W.,
Washington 20006. Through regional offices, the Association can
give on-the-spot community service in conducting studies of recreation and park resources and needs; in acquiring open space, planning
its use, and protecting it from encroachment.

League of Women Voters of the United States, 1200 17th Street, N.W.,
Washington 20036. Its publication "Land and Water for Tomorrow" (free) is a valuable handbook for training community leaders
for conservation activities.

American Planning and Civic Assoc., 901 Union Trust Building, Washington 20005. Its purpose is to advise on land use and community improvement.

The Nature Conservancy (1946), 1522 K Street, N.W., Washington 20005. A membership corporation dedicated to the preservation of natural areas. It cooperates with other agencies to acquire lands for scientific and educational purposes, and will be interested in any efforts to establish such areas.

National Audubon Society, 1130 Fifth Avenue, New York 10028. Its *Audubon Magazine,* appearing bimonthly, is an excellent source of material not only on birds but on nature in its many aspects; even the advertisements will be found useful to the person with land at the rural fringes. Membership $10.00 per year. The Society is aggressively active in conservation affairs, fosters sanctuaries, bird study tours and camps, and maintains an agency for nature center development.

National Wildlife Federation. 1412 16th Street, N.W., Washington 20036. Its *Conservation News,* weekly, is an excellent review of current affairs dealing with this interest. Another of its periodicals, *National Wildlife,* is one of America's handsomest and contains articles of interest on wildlife. Bimonthly. Membership $5.00 annually.

Private Organizations, Local and Regional

League of Women Voters, local chapters. Often cooperative in conservation endeavors for public good.

Horticultural Societies, state branches. Are usually actively interested in roadside improvements, and other matters that recognize the relation of man to the land.

Audubon Societies. Active at state and local levels. Many publish their own journals; sponsor sanctuaries, nature centers, bird study walks, conservation activities.

Museums of Natural History. Where available, they may provide authoritative help in landowners' problems dealing with living things; conduct educational programs; publish helpful books, pamphlets, and periodicals. Many have membership categories with programs and privileges. Some have municipal or county support. All are, at least to a degree, dependent on community-wide support.

Youth Organizations. The Boy Scouts, Girl Scouts, and Campfire Girls have strong interests in the availability of natural lands for educational and recreational purposes. They may be expected to give moral support in any endeavor aimed at preserving or improving natural resources.

Identification, Plants and Animals

No institution has competence in identification of all plants and animals, but for most purposes there will probably be someone in any natural history museum who can be of help, either providing the identification or advising where it may be found. County Extension Agents can usually help on matters of troublesome insect pests or plant diseases. Plant identification questions, if of a specialized nature, should be referred to the curator of the herbarium of a museum or university with such a collection. The person making the inquiry, however, should realize that individuals in charge of collections are heavily burdened with such questions and their time should not be requested for trivial matters.

Forest Tree Planting, Harvest, Care

Advice may be sought from your County Agricultural Agent, the nearest office of the Forest Service, or the State Forester, the latter usually on the staff of the Conservation Department. If there is a School of Forestry nearby, one might seek professional advice from a faculty member. Forestry schools are:

Harvard School of Forestry, Petersham, Mass.

Yale School of Forestry, New Haven, Conn.

School of Forestry, University of Michigan, Ann Arbor.

New York State School of Forestry, Syracuse University, Syracuse, N. Y.

Tree Selection for the Home Grounds

A reliable nurseryman familiar with local conditions is a proper point of contact, and tree services should also have practical suggestions (see the Yellow Pages in your phone directory). Arboretums and managers of public parks could help too. For specific suggestions in print refer to the titles in Appendix B.

Animal Control

Call your local Conservation Department officer if the problem is with a game or fur bearing animal. In the case of unprotected animals which may be pests, see your County Agricultural Extension Agent.

Bird Study

Go to your nearest natural history museum, nature center, university zoology department, or library to find the address of the headquarters of your state or local Audubon society. The National Audubon Society can also provide such information.

Bird and Mammal Control Services and Supplies

Traps:
   Havahart, 158–A Water Street, Ossining, N. Y. 10562. Humane live traps, several sizes. Trapping guide and price list on request.
Sound Devices:
   B. M. Lawrence and Co., 24 California St., San Francisco, Calif. 94111. A portable unit of Klaxon horns with batteries.
   Jennings Industries, Inc. 2730 Chanticleer Ave., Santa Cruz, Calif. 95060. Sound recordings of alarm notes of species of birds that are nuisances when in flocks, particularly in roosts, orchards, airports. Audio equipment available.

For Plate Glass Warning or to Discourage Roosting

Whirling Novelties:
   The Bower Co., 8440 Warner Dr., Culver City, Calif. 94601. 20-foot reinforced streamers, by the dozen.
   Germain's, Inc., P. O. Box 3233, Los Angeles, Calif. 90054. 10 flying disks in a package.
Protective Netting:
   Bemis Bros. Bag Co., Visinet Mill, 2400 S. 2nd St., St. Louis, Mo. 63104. Plastic paper, 1/2 inch openings, widths 40 and 80 feet.
   Chicopee Manufacturing Co., Lumite Division, Cornelia, Ga. 30531. Lumite Saran shade cloth is one type.
   Moodus Net & Twine, Inc., Moodus, Conn. 06469. Nylon, 1 inch openings, widths of 9 and 18 feet.
   Nichols Net and Twine, R.R. 3, Bend Rd., East St. Louis, Ill. 62201. Various types of cotton or nylon netting.
   Union Carbide Corp., Plastics Div., 270 Park Ave., New York, N.Y. 10017. One type is polyethylene netting, 1 inch openings, 84 ft. wide, 300 ft long.
Revolving Lights:
   Bird-X, Inc., 325 West Huron St., Chicago, Ill. 60610
   R. E. Dietz Co., 225 Wilkinson St., Syracuse, N. Y. 13201

The Huge Co., 884–6 Hodiamont Ave., St. Louis, Mo. 63112
Trippe Manufacturing Co., 133 N. Jefferson St., Chicago, Ill. 60606

Pesticides and Herbicides

This is a field fraught with prejudice and passion. Some government agencies and university departments have shown themselves to be heavily biased, depending on whether their first interests are in trees, crops, public health, or birds. It is suggested that you refer to appropriate literature cited in Appendix B. This material cannot be thoroughly up to date, for the field is rapidly changing. New products, new applications, and new data adverse to their use, appear with frequency. Best advice, perhaps, is to avoid the use of chemicals in the environment, though it may cost you some discomfort and possibly a tree or two.

Instruction

State universities, many school systems, community houses, and natural science museums offer adult education courses in matters pertaining to the fields on which this book touches. Some are offered for credit, some are noncredit. Watch your local press for announcements or, better, ask your local educational organizations to send you listings of present courses.

Maps, Charts, Aerial Photographs

U. S. Geological Survey, Map Information Office, Department of the Interior, Washington 20242. Topographic sheets with contour lines, cultural features, etc., in scale of 1:24,000. State lists available.

United States Lake Survey, Federal Building, Cleveland, Ohio
Charts of Great Lakes shore areas. Lists available.

Coast and Geodetic Survey, U. S. Department of Commerce, Washington. Coastal charts.

U. S. Army Map Service, Corps of Engineers, Washington. Coastal charts.

Soil Conservation Service, U.S. Department of Agriculture, Washington 20250. County soil charts and reports. Lists of available charts on request. Aerial photographs of the entire area have been made and are available for purchase at different degrees of enlargement. Sets for each county are on file either with the Soil Conservation officer in the county or with the County Agricultural Agent.

Some county agencies have prepared highly specialized maps dealing with regional planning and recreational development. Inquiry may prove rewarding.

Appendix B.

This reading list has been checked to September 1967. To that time all titles were in print and at prices stated. Book dealers will process orders to better known publishers. Publications of the United States Government are available from the Government Printing Office, for which remittance (no stamps) with order is required.

The Golden Nature Guides, priced at $1.00, are also available in cloth bound editions.

All recommended manuals are well illustrated.

Addresses of Non-commercial Publishers Whose Books or Pamphlets may be Ordered Directly.

Cranbrook Institute of Science, Bloomfield Hills, Michigan 48013

National Audubon Society, 1130 Fifth Avenue, New York, N.Y. 10028

National Geographic Society, 1145 17th Street N. W., Washington, D. C. 20036

National Wildlife Federation, 1412 16th Street N. W., Washington, D. C. 20036

Resources for the Future. Their publications distributed by The Johns Hopkins Press, Baltimore, Maryland 21218

Superintendent of Documents, U.S. Government Printing Office, Washington, D.C. 20402

Chapter 1. From Wilderness to Subdivision.

Carson, Rachel. 1962. Silent Spring. Houghton Mifflin, 368 pp., cloth $5.95, paperback 75 cents.

Clepper, H. E. (ed.). 1966. Origins of American conservation. Ronald Press, 203 pp., $3.75.

Munzer, Martha E. 1964. Planning our town. Random House, 180 pp., $3.95.

Rudd, Robert. 1966. Pesticides and the living landscape. Univ. Wisc., 320 pp., $1.95.

Swift, Ernest. 1958. The glory trail; the great American migration and its impact on natural resources. Nat. Wildlife Fed., 50 pp., single copy free, additional copies 25 cents.

Chapter 2. The Site and the Soil

Anderson, W. L. 1965. Making land produce useful wildlife. USDA Farmers' Bull. No. 2035, 30 pp., 15 cents.

Barrett, Paul M. 1949. Conserving soil by better land-use practices. Mich. St. Univ. Coop. Ext. Serv. (East Lansing) Bull. 203. 32 pp., free.

Callison, C. H. (rev. ed.). 1967. America's natural resources. Ronald Press, 220 pp., $5.00.

Farb. P. 1959. Living earth. Harper & Bros., 178 pp., $3.95.

Herber, L. 1962. Our synthetic environment. Knopf, 285 pp., $4.95.

Hockensmith, R. D., and J. G. Steele. 1962. Soil erosion—the work of uncontrolled water. USDA Information Bull. 260, 16 pp., 10 cents.

Klingebiel, A. A. 1967. Know the soil you build on. USDA Information Bull. 320, 16 pp., 15 cents.

Marsh, G. P. 1965. Man and nature. Harvard Univ., 502 pp., $7.95.

Morgan, R. J. 1966. Governing soil conservation. Resources for the Future, Johns Hopkins Press, 399 pp., $8.00.

Osborn, R. O. 1963. Soil conservation at home; tips for city and suburban dwellers. USDA Information Bull. 244, 32 pp., 20 cents.

Russell, E. John. 1957. The world of the soil. Collins, London, 237 pp., $6.00.

U.S. Dept. of Agric. Soil. Yearbook for 1957. 784 pp., $2.25.

———— Land. Yearbook for 1958. 605 pp., $2.25.

———— A place to live. Yearbook for 1963. 584 pp., $3.00.

———— 1965. The American outdoors. Misc. Publ. No. 1000, 77 pp., 55 cents.

Whyte, W. H. 1959. Securing open space for urban America: Conservation easements. Urban Land Inst. Tech. Bull. No. 36. 67 pp., $3.00.

————1964. Cluster development. Amer. Conserv. Assoc., 30 Rockefeller Plaza, N.Y. 130 pp., hard cover $6.00, paper $4.00.

Chapter 3. Water On and Under Your Land

Neely, W. W., Davison, Verne E., and Compton, Lawrence V. 1965. Warm water ponds for fishing. USDA Farmers' Bull. 2210, 16 pp., 10 cents.

U.S. Dept. Agric. Water. Yearbook for 1955, 751 pp., $2.00.

Chapter 4. Vegetation, High and Low

Anderson, Wallace L. 1960. Making land produce useful wildlife. USDA Farmers' Bull. 2035, 30 pp., 15 cents.

Anderson, W. L., and F. C. Edminster. 1954. The multiflora rose for fences and wildlife. USDA Leaflet No. 374, 8 pp., 5 cents.

Billington, Cecil. 1968. Shrubs of Michigan, 2nd ed., 2nd printing. Cranbrook Inst. Sci., 339 pp., $4.50.

———— 1952. Ferns of Michigan. Cranbrook Inst. Sci., 248 pp., $5.00 Essentially complete for northeastern United States.

Crooks, D. M., L. W. Kephart and D. L. Klingman. 1963. Poison-ivy, poison oak, and poison sumac: identification, precautions, eradication. USDA Farmers' Bull. No. 1972, 27 pp., 15 cents.

Illinois Nat. Hist. Survey. 1965. Careful with that tree. Urbana, Ill., 61803, 4 pp., free.

Kingsbury, J. M. 1964. Poisonous plants of the United States and Canada. Prentice-Hall, 626 pp., $13.00.

McAtee, W. L. 1936. Groups of plants valuable for wildlife utilization and erosion control. USDA Circular No. 412, 12 pp., 5 cents.

McKenny, Margaret. 1962. The savory wild mushroom. Univ. of Wisc., 133 pp., $3.95.

Miller, H. C., and S. B. Silverborg. 1967. Maple tree problems. N.Y. State Tree Pest Publ. F-12, State Univ. Coll. of Forestry, Syracuse, N.Y. 13210, 25 pp., free.

Morgan, R. J. 1965. Governing soil conservation. Resources for the Future, from Johns Hopkins Press, 413 pp., $8.00.

Pomerleau, R., and H. A. C. Jackson. 1951. Mushrooms of Eastern Canada and the United States. Editions Chantecler, Montreal, or Stechert, 302 pp., $7.50.

St. John, John (ed.). 1961. The golden guide to lawns, trees, and shrubs. Golden Press, 176 pp., $1.00.

Schery, Robert W. 1963. The householder's guide to outdoor beauty. Pocket Books, 337 pp., 50 cents.

Smith, Alexander H. 1963. The mushroom hunter's field guide. Univ. of Mich. Press, 264 pp., $6.95.

Smith, Helen V. 1966. Michigan wildflowers (rev. ed.). Cranbrook Inst. Sci., 477 pp., $6.00.

Steffek, E. F. 1954. Wild flowers and how to grow them. Crown Publishers (419 Fourth Ave., New York 10016), 192 pp., illus., $3.95.

Stoddard, C. H. 1961. The small private forest in the United States. Resources for the Future, from Johns Hopkins Press, 171 pp., $2.00.

U.S. Dept. of Agric. Trees. Yearbook for 1949. 944 pp., $2.00.

_____1963. Maple diseases and their control. Home and Garden Bull. No. 81, 8 pp., 5 cents.

_____1967. A guide to natural beauty. Misc. Publ. No. 1056, 33 pp., 36 color pls., 55 cents.

Wallner, W. E., and J. H. Hart. 1965. Dutch elm disease control. Mich. State Univ. Extension Bull. 506, East Lansing., 6 pp., free.

Chapter 5. Neighbors in Furs.

Burkholder, B. L. 1955. Control of small predators. U. S. Dept. Interior, Fish and Wildlife Serv. Circ. 33, 7 pp., 5 cents.

Burt, W. H., and R. B. Grossenherder. 1964. A field guide to the mammals. Houghton Mifflin, 222 pp., $4.95.

Cahalane, V. 1953. The mammals of North America. Macmillan, 682 pp., $7.95.

Hamilton, W. J. 1936. Rats and their control. Cornell Extension Bull. 353, N.Y. State College of Agric. at Cornell Univ., Ithaca, N. Y., 32 pp., free.

Moore, C. B. 1954. The book of wild pets. Chas. Brantford Co., Boston, 577 pp., $6.50.

Murie, O. 1954. A field guide to animal tracks. Houghton Mifflin, 398 pp., $4.95.

Palmer, R. S. 1954. The mammal guide. Doubleday, 384 pp., $5.50.

Silver, J. 1941. Mole control. U. S. Dept. Int., Fish and Wildl Serv. Conservation Bull. 16, 17 pp., 10 cents.

Silver, J., W. E. Crouch and M. C. Betts. 1942. Rat proofing buildings and premises. U. S. Dept. Interior, Fish and Wildlife Serv. Conservation Bull. 19, 26 pp., 10 cents.

Zim, H. S., and D. F. Hoffmeister. 1955. Mammals; a guide to familiar American species. Simon & Schuster, 160 pp., cloth $3.95, paper $1.00.

Chapter 6. Of Bird Life.

Berger, A. J. 1961. Bird study. Wiley, 389 pp., $8.25.

Cruickshank, A. D. 1953. Pocket guide to birds; Eastern and Central North

America. Washington Square, 216 pp., 50 cents.

Cruickshank, A. D. and H. G. 1958. 1001 questions answered about birds. Dodd, Mead & Co., 291 pp., $6.00.

Darling, L. and L. 1962. Bird. Houghton Mifflin, 261 pp., $5.00.

Davison, Verne E. 1965. Lespedezas for quail and good land use. U.S. Dept. Agric. Leaflet No. 373, 8 pp., 5 cents.

——— 1967. Attracting birds from the prairies to the Atlantic. Crowell, 269 pp., $6.95.

Laboratory of Ornithology, Cornell University, Ithaca, N.Y.

Bird songs in your garden. A 10-inch 33 ⅓ rpm record album. 31 full color photographs. $6.95.

Field guide to bird songs. Two 12-inch LP records. Designed to accompany Peterson's Field Guide to the Birds. $10.95.

American bird songs, Vol. I, 60 species; Vol. II, 51 species. $7.75 each.

Songbirds of America. $6.95.

An evening in sapsucker woods. 32 species. $4.95.

Music and bird songs. $5.00.

Dawn in a duck blind. $5.00.

McKenny, M. 1939. Birds in the garden and how to attract them. Reynal & Hitchcock, 349 pp., $4.95.

Nagel, Werner. Habitat improvement: key to game abundance. Nat. Wildlife Fed., No. A-6, 24 pp., 10 cents.

Niering, W. A., and R. H. Goodwin. 1963. Creating new landscapes with herbicides; a homeowner's guide. Connecticut Arboretum Bull. No. 14, Conn. College, New London 06320, 30 pp., $1.00.

Peterson, Roger Tory. 1947. A field guide to the birds. Houghton Mifflin, 314 pp., $4.95.

——— Bird houses and feeders. Nat. Audubon Soc. Circ. 29, 12 pp., 5 cents.

Pough, R. H. 1946. Audubon bird guide. Eastern land birds. Doubleday, 354 pp., $4.95.

——— 1951. Water bird guide. Doubleday, 352 pp., $3.50.

Robbins, C. S., B. Bruun, and H. S. Zim. 1966. Birds of North America; a guide to field identification. Golden Press, 340 pp., cloth $4.50, paper $2.95.

Sawyer, E. J. 1969. Homes for wildlife; how to make and where to place them. Cranbrook Inst. Sci., ca. 50 pp., ca. 75 cents.

Terres, J. 1953. Song birds in your garden. Thos. Crowell, N.Y., 274 pp., $3.95.

Van Tyne, J., and A. Berger. 1965. Fundamentals of ornithology. Wiley, 624 pp., $10.50.

Wetmore, A., and others. 1965. Song and garden birds of North America. Includes phonograph records with 70 of the most musical songsters. Nat. Geographic Soc., 400 pp., 544 illus., $11.95.

——— 1965. Water, prey and game birds of North America. Includes an album of six high-fidelity records, sounds of 97 species. Nat. Geographic Soc., 464 pp., $11.95.

Zim, H. S., and I. N. Gabrielson. 1949. Birds; a guide to the most familiar American birds. Golden Press, 155 pp., $1.00.

Chapter 7. Snakes, Turtles, Toads, and Fish

Conant, R. 1958. A field guide to the reptiles and amphibians of Eastern North America. Houghton Mifflin, 366 pp., $4.95.

Kellogg, P. R., and A. A. Allen. Voices of the night. 12-inch LP record of 34 frogs and toads of the United States and Canada. Laboratory of Ornithology, Cornell Univ., $6.75.

Lagler, Karl F. 1956. Freshwater fishery biology. Brown, 421 pp., $7.50.

Pope, C. H. 1937. Snakes alive. Viking, 238 pp., $5.00.

Zim, H. S., and H. M. Smith. 1956. Reptiles and amphibians. Simon & Schuster, Golden Press, 100 pp., cloth $3.95, paper $1.00.

Chapter 8. The Lower Animals.

Cottam, Dr. Clarence. Chemical pesticides—a national problem. National Wildlife Fed., A-8, 10 pp. Single copy free, additional 10 cents each.

Curran, C. H. 1951. Insects in your life. Sheridan House, N.Y., 316 pp., $6.00.

English, L. L. 1962. Illinois trees and shrubs; their insect enemies. Ill. Nat. Hist. Survey Circ. 47, Urbana, Ill. 61801, 92 pp., $1.00.

Fichter, G. S. 1966. Insect pests. Golden Press, 160 pp., $1.00.

Fluno, J. H. 1965. Controlling mosquitoes in your home and on your premises. USDA Home and Garden Bull. No. 84, 12 pp., 10 cents.

Karston, R. J. 1953. The spiders. W. E. Brown Co., Dubuque, Iowa, 226 pp., $2.50.

Lougee, L. B. 1964. The web of the spider. Cranbrook Inst. Sci., 44 pp., $3.50.

Peairs, L. M., and R. H. Davidson. Insect pests of farm, garden, and orchard, 5th ed. Wiley, 568 pp., $9.25.

Randolph, T. G. 1962. Human ecology and susceptibility to the chemical environment. C. C. Thomas, Springfield, Ill., 148 pp., $6.50.

Swain, R. B. 1948. The insect guide. Doubleday, 309 pp., $4.95.

U.S. Dept. of Agric. 1963. Ants in the home and garden; how to control them. USDA Home and Garden Bull. No. 28, 11 pp., 10 cents.

———— 1964. Handbook 120, 207 pp., $1.00. Insecticide recommendations of the Entomology Research Division.

Zim, H. S., and Clarence Cottam. 1951. Insects; a guide to familiar American insects. Simon & Schuster, Golden Press, 157 pp., cloth $3.95, paper $1.00.

Chapter 9. Community Affairs and Yours.

Ashbaugh, B. L. 1963. Planning a nature center. Nature Centers Division, National Audubon Soc., 88 pp., $2.00.

———— 1965. Trail planning and layout. National Audubon Soc., 104 pp., $2.50.

Headley, J. C., and J. H. Lewis. 1967. The pesticide problem; an economic approach to public policy. Resources for the Future, from Johns Hopkins Press, 141 pp., $3.50.

Herfindahl, O. C., and A. V. Kneese. 1965. Quality of the environment. Resources for the Future, from Johns Hopkins Press, 96 pp., $2.00.

Crowe, S., and Z. Miller (editors). 1964. The landscape architect's role in the changing landscape. (Vol. 2 of "Shaping Tomorrow's Landscape.") Djambatan, Amsterdam, Holland. Ca. 70 pp., $10.40.

Index to selected outdoor recreation literature, 1966. 1967. Vol. I, Bureau of Outdoor Recreation and Dept. of Int. Library, 154 pp., 75 cents.

Morton, D. 1962. Wildlife sanctuaries. Audubon Center of Greenwich, Conn., Publ. 1. 24 pp., 50 cents.

Open Space Action Committee. 1965. Stewardship: the land, the landowner, the metropolis. 145 East 52nd St., N.Y. 10022. 82 pp., hard cover $6.00, soft cover $3.00.

——————— 1967. Open space preservation methods. 80 pp., $2.00.

Siegel, S. A. 1960. The law of open space. Regional Plan Assoc., 230 W. 41st St., New York 10036. 72 pp., $3.50. Legal aspects of acquiring or otherwise preserving open space in the tri-state New York Metropolitan Region.

Sukloff, Hyman. 1965. Small property owners' legal guide. Arco Publ. Co., 219 Park Ave. S., New York.

Tunnard, C., and B. Pushkarev. 1963. Man-made America, chaos or control? Yale Univ. Press, 479 pp., $15.00.

U.S. Dept. of Agric. 1965. Community improvement through beautification. 8 pp., 5 cents.

Whyte, William H. 1962. Open space action, *in* Outdoor Recreation Resources Review Commission Study Report No. 15. U.S. Government Printing Office, 128 pp., $2.00.

Index

The numbers in italics are the numbers of photographs that will be found in a section between pages 56 and 57.

Drawings, for the most part, are not indexed as their page numbers would be the same as, or close to, the references for the subject in the text.